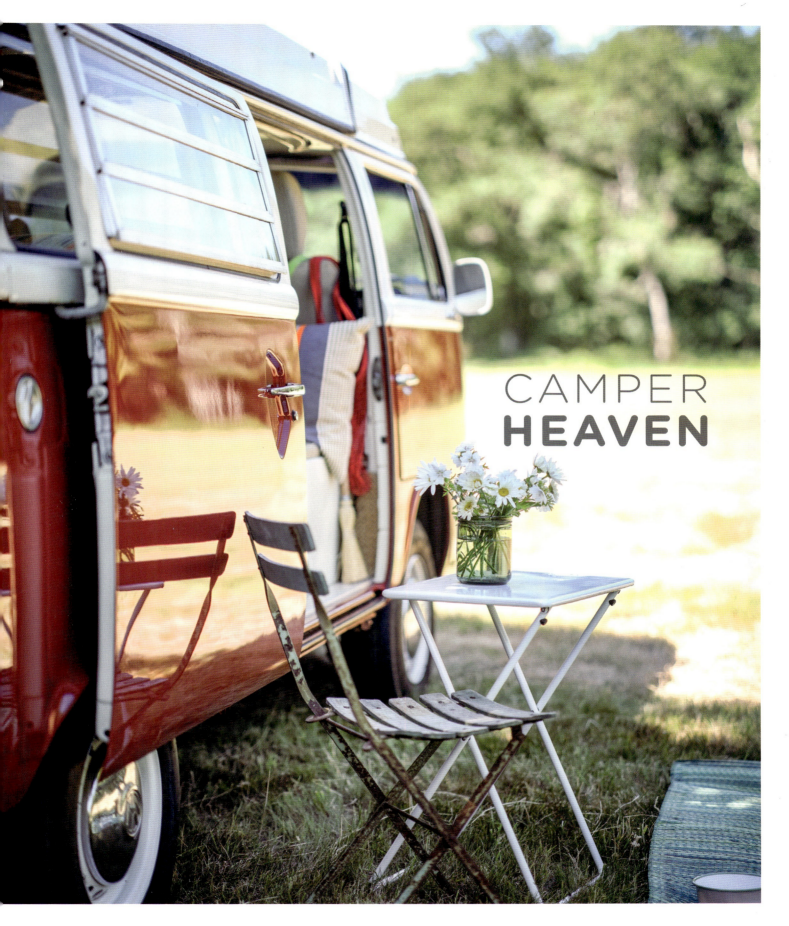

CAMPER
**HEAVEN**

# CAMPER HEAVEN

## VAN LIFE ON THE OPEN ROAD

DEE CAMPLING

With photography by
**DAN DUCHARS**

**CICO BOOKS**

LONDON  NEW YORK

**Senior designer**  Toni Kay
**Senior commissioning editor**
  Annabel Morgan
**Editor**  Sophie Devlin
**Location research**  Jess Walton
**Head of production**  Patricia Harrington
**Art director**  Sally Powell
**Creative director**  Leslie Harrington

For photography credits and copyright
information, see page 172.

Published in 2023 by CICO Books
An imprint of Ryland Peters & Small Ltd

20–21 Jockey's Fields
London WC1R 4BW

341 E 116th St
New York, NY 10029

www.rylandpeters.com

10 9 8 7 6 5 4 3 2 1

Text © Dee Campling 2023
Design © CICO Books 2023

A CIP catalog record for this book is
available from the Library of Congress
and the British Library.

ISBN 978-1-80065-121-0

Printed in China

MIX
Paper from
responsible sources
FSC® C106563

# CONTENTS

# INTRODUCTION

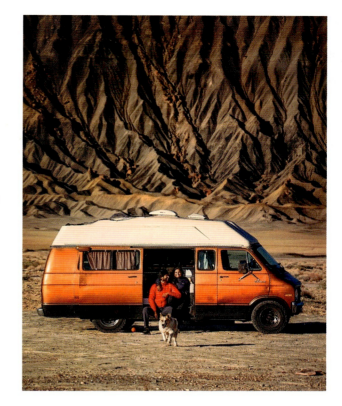

I have always been particularly inspired by interiors that manage the twin feat of serving as a beautiful personal sanctuary in addition to being highly practical and adaptable. I love the idea of creating a space where you can feel entirely at home, yet everything within it is flexible and multi-purpose. And, of course, the beautiful place itself should ideally be suitable for more than one use – especially now that so many of us have begun to carve out space for working from home.

In recent years, self-built camper vans have boomed in popularity as more people have become aware of the many possibilities they offer. After all, a well-designed camper is a home-from-home. You can create an entirely personal, aesthetically pleasing yet functional space for living, sleeping, working, eating and more. And when it is parked on your driveway, it can become an extension of your house and then you can drive it away to take in a new experience, a new adventure or even just a new view.

In the pages that follow, I will take you through my own journey toward owning and creating a tiny home on wheels, as well as the experiences of 12 other owners of camper vans, each of whom has taken a vehicle – whether it be a brand-new panel van, a vintage vehicle, a former horsebox or even a fire truck – and turned it into a camper van that has enabled them to fulfil their dreams around living, working and travelling.

This book is not a practical guide on how to build a camper van, rather a look at how owners have designed interiors that meet their various needs and express their personalities. It is an insight into how they have decided their priorities and considered their core style, the materials available to them and their own practical skills. They have each styled their own inspiring version of a sanctuary – their camper heaven.

# A HISTORY
# OF VAN LIFE

LEFT *This Dormobile conversion of a Bedford CA van is from 1959 and was one of the first to include a pop-up roof. Dormobile was the leading British converter of camper vans between the 1950s and 1970s, and even became the generic name in the UK for camper vans in the 1960s.*

BELOW *The Ford Thames 400E van was popular with camper converters thanks to its square shape and the size of its engine, which was larger than those of its contemporaries.*

## IN THE BEGINNING

Camper vans enable so many people to take to the road and enjoy freedom. It's no surprise, after a pandemic when other modes of travel were limited for all of us, that they're more popular now than ever. There is a van for everyone's budget – big or small, old or new – and the option to customize one to your specifications is very appealing.

The very first 'motorized caravan' to hit the market was developed by the Eccles Motor Transport Company. It went on sale in 1919, just after the First World War. However, the rising popularity of the car-pulled caravan stalled development of motorized camper vans, and by the Second World War, the idea had faded.

## HIPPIE HEYDAY

At the start of the 1950s, production of the first pressed-steel vans began and this was enough to kick-start the dormant camper van market. The German caravan maker Westfalia started selling a kit conversion for the iconic Volkswagen Bus, and in the UK, Dormobile began selling a converted Bedford CA van with a pop-up roof.

The late 1950s saw the launch of Ford's Thames 400E van, which was particularly attractive to converters

because of its 1.6-litre engine. Morris brought out the J4 in the early 1960s, and throughout the decade, other commercial vans made by Austin and Commer became the top choices to convert for specialist firms such as Devon Conversions, Auto-Sleepers and Airborne, among others. Also during this period, a law was passed in the UK that excluded motorhomes from the category of commercial vehicles, meaning they were legally on a par with private cars and were no longer subject to a reduced speed limit. This new status gave the camper van even broader appeal and the market expanded accordingly. In 1967, the Volkswagen T2 was introduced and it is still a powerful emblem of 1960s counterculture.

LEFT  Based in Dorset, south-west England, Caravans International (Motorised) began selling camper van conversions in the 1960s, as well as caravans made by Sprite, Eccles, Fairholme and B Europe.

BELOW  A 1969 advert for a Dormobile conversion of a Ford Transit Mark 1. The van's interior featured innovatons such as the 'Dormatic' seat, which folded down into a bed, and a hob/stovetop that could be stowed away when on the move.

## Dormobile Enterprise

LEFT  A Dormobile conversion of an Austin Morris J4 from 1966. Dormobile dominated Britain's van conversion market in the 1960s, and its signature red-striped pop-up roof was a familiar sight on campsites throughout the UK.

OPPOSITE *This 1978 Volkswagen T2, originally converted by Westfalia, belongs to Emma and Jeremy Bates (see pages 86–95). Although the interior has been replaced, the layout remains the same – a testament to its innovative design.*

BELOW *A 1973 Auto-Sleeper conversion of a Bedford CF van. Auto-Sleeper was founded in 1961 by the Trevelyan family, who went into business after first building their own camper based on a Morris J2 van.*

BELOW RIGHT *A 1971 advert for the Danbury Conversions take on a Volkswagen T2, with the option of forward-facing passenger seats. Versatility was a big selling point for camper vans in the mid to late 20th century, just as it is now.*

At the same time, the army began to use converted long-wheelbase Land Rovers as camper vans for its officers during training exercises. Known as Carawagons, these were fitted out with a fold-up bed, a plotting table and a sink for army use – or with four berths for civilians wishing to tour off the beaten track. The rise of wild camping strengthened the ties between camper vans and 'hippie' subcultures.

## FORM MEETS FUNCTION

By the 1970s, the Ford Transit had been launched with its larger space and modern cab. Firms such as Dormobile were able to convert the Transit with great success and it became a top seller. At the other end of the market were micro-campers such as the Canterbury, which was based on the Ford Escort estate car. Throughout the 1970s, camper vans proved as popular as ever and were a great alternative to larger coach-built motorhomes such as the Bedford Bedouin, as they were easier to park and drive. However, in 1973, VAT introduction and the oil crisis hit the camper van market, and by the early 1980s, many converters had gone out of business.

A few survived, though, and in 1979 the new Volkswagen T3 became another popular base vehicle. Camper specifications also improved with the addition of hot-water systems and mains power. Fitted fridges and cookers also became the norm.

The best of both worlds

Danbury Conversions offer you the best of both worlds. An economical vehicle for everyday use, with built-in comfort and unequalled mobility ... ideal for town or country, PLUS all the amenities of a luxury caravan. Danbury Conversions offer you "FORWARD FACING SEATS" – do away with that crick in the neck – here is the opportunity to go where and when you please in comfort.

**Danbury** CONVERSIONS LTD
DANBURY CONVERSIONS LTD.
Danbury, Chelmsford, Essex.
Tel: Danbury 2224/7.

BELOW  A 1977 advert for a Devon Conversions Volkswagen T3. Founded in 1956, Devon was one of the pioneers of van conversions. The Devon LT was built for comfort and featured a double bed, a 1.8m/6ft bunk, a full-height hot and cold shower, a proper oven and hob/stovetop and a heater.

RIGHT  A 1978 Devon Caravette based on the Volkswagen T2. Like many of its competitors, Devon Conversions was started by skilled enthusiasts. Its founder Jack White was a builder and carpenter with a passion for Volkswagen vehicles. In 1960, the firm employed 75 local tradesmen to produce 1,000 Caravettes a year.

With new longer-wheelbase vans appearing on the market such as the Renault Trafic, bathrooms could be placed at the rear of the camper, allowing more space in the living areas. Mercedes vans, popular since the 1970s, continue to be sought after with the Mercedes-Benz Sprinter being one of the most common vans for conversion today.

The 1980s to the 2000s heralded the arrival of converters such as Trigano and La Strada. New base vehicles including the Volkswagen T4, T5 and Crafter offered greater comfort and a more car-like driving experience than their predecessors. These improvements have made camper vans even more appealing in recent years. The growth of the Internet and its multitude of how-to videos has also meant that converting a van yourself is easier than ever. At the same time, the popularity of social-media platforms such as Instagram has spread the word and made van life look both aspirational and attainable.

*RIGHT  A 1996 Auto-Sleepers Trident built on a Volkswagen T4. The high-top roof is a clever design element that allows the owner to fully stand up inside the camper van – an important consideration that is often overlooked.*

*BELOW  A 2003 Volkswagen advert for the T4 California built by Westfalia invites you to 'Spend the Weekend at Home', emphasizing the 'home-from-home' aspect of camper ownership.*

## Spend the Weekend at Home

Living with a Volkswagen has never been so easy or pleasurable. Versatile enough to meet a wide range of needs, you're as likely to see it on the school run as at the golf club or on a caravan park. With all the essentials of home, your weekends may never be the same again.

All new van conversions include: electric windows and mirrors, cab seat arm rests, colour coded bumpers and mirror housings, central locking and stylish wheel trims.

Not only are our van conversions both attractive and comfortable, the reliability and build quality of our motorhomes are supplemented with a standard 3 year base vehicle warranty* and 3 year Volkswagen Emergency Assistance.

So the choice is yours. Whether travelling near or far, with family, friends, or just your walking boots, we believe that you'll always feel at home with a Volkswagen. To find out more, contact your local Volkswagen Motorhome dealer.

To receive the latest Volkswagen Motorhome brochure, simply call

### 0800 71 71 31

VW VOLKSWAGEN Motorhomes

## A NEW ERA

So here we are 100 years after the invention of the very first camper van with a rich history of van conversion behind us. There are so many vintage and modern vehicles to choose from, and much inspiration and expertise to draw on. Many of the classic vehicles have survived to this day, and the original Volkswagen Buses, the T1 and T2, are still icons of the camper van world.

Camper vans are now much more than just a means of getting an inexpensive holiday. They have developed into homes on wheels, which many owners have designed and decorated to suit their personal style. As the cost of home ownership continues to be out of reach for many people, a few van lifers are embracing the possibilities of the nomadic lifestyle and opting to live in their vehicles full time. The boundaries of what you can do with camper van designs and layouts, and how you can use them, are being pushed all the time.

All the camper vans featured in this book have enabled their owners to embark on new adventures, myself included. It's no surprise that these wonderful vehicles are now more popular than ever.

# WHAT IS A CAMPER VAN?

FAR LEFT & LEFT *After successfully converting a former ambulance into a camper van (see opposite and pages 56–67), DIY expert Max McMurdo set his sights on creating a camper out of the smallest vehicle he could think of – a Smart car. Affectionately nicknamed 'The Scamper', the miniature van sleeps two people in the roof tent, and the boot/trunk folds open to reveal a tiny kitchen.*

OPPOSITE *Steph Rhodes and Matt H-B's 1985 Mercedes-Benz Vario 613D, which they have named Sandy, was once a police truck (top left; see pages 138–149). Joseph and Sian Orpen drive a former horsebox with Japanese-style wooden cladding (top right; see pages 114–129). Emma and Jeremy Bates's iconic Volkswagen T2 (bottom left; see pages 86–95). Max McMurdo's converted ambulance (bottom right; see pages 56–67).*

There are so many different varieties of camper vans and motorhomes out there that it can be hard to tell which is which, but in a nutshell, a camper van is a panel van made by a manufacturer such as Ford or Volkswagen, that has then been converted into a camper van.

**Camper vans can then be broken down into three main types:**

**1** *Those that have been made in-house by the original manufacturer, such as the Volkswagen California and the Mercedes-Benz Marco Polo in the UK and the Mercedes-Benz Metris Weekender and Airstream Interstate 19 in the US.*
**2** *Those panel vans that have been converted by specialist companies, such as Devon Conversions and Danbury in the UK and Sportsmobile and Vanworks in the US.*
**3** *Those that have been converted by private individuals.*

Camper vans are different to motorhomes in so far as the latter can be much larger and more luxurious inside, and are typically built from the inside out before being placed onto the cutaway chassis of a large van or bus.

When people think of a camper van, the classic Volkswagen Microbus often springs to mind. However, what many people don't know is that the company did not make its California camper vans in-house until 2003. Up to that point, and since 1951, all authorized VW camper conversions had been done by the specialist company Westfalia. In-house camper vans are usually created to a high standard, in line with the manufacturer's brand values and customer profile. The conversion to a camper van is a standard design with some upgrade options.

If you want a more bespoke camper, a conversion company could help. Some will convert a van to their own design, some will work with you to realize your own design and many will do a hybrid of both. Some conversion companies only work with vans made by certain brands.

Steph and Matt opted for a substantial kitchen in their camper van, as they live in it full time. Alternatively, you may prioritize a larger kitchen just because you're a foodie, even if you only use it on a part-time basis. The boho interior of this van pays homage to California's laid-back surf culture, especially the idea of a surf shack.

Others will take any van that you have sourced yourself and work with you to design and build the conversion. The most cost-effective option is to do the conversion yourself to avoid the cost of labour – this will also give you total control over the design, layout and feel of the interior. Before you start, though, there are a number of things to consider.

Firstly, how many people will be sleeping in the van? A small van such as a Volkswagen Caddy will sleep two people, a medium van such as a Ford Transit will sleep two to four and a large van such as a Mercedes-Benz Sprinter will sleep up to six, depending on the configuration. Don't forget that adding a pop-up roof will give you room for two additional berths without compromising on space.

Secondly, is having a bathroom essential to you? If you are accommodating more than two people and you require a bathroom, then you will probably need a long-wheelbase version of one of the popular medium-to-large vans. You will also need to scale up your water storage.

Thirdly, would you prefer a fixed bed or one that folds out from the seating? The beauty of a fixed bed is that it's ready and made for you as soon as you park up. On the other hand, the fold-out bed option saves space, but it may be less comfortable and it can feel inconvenient to fold out and make up the bed every night. Another aspect to consider is the size of the kitchen. Do you want a fully equipped kitchen or a more compact but less functional design? This depends I think on whether you are planning on living in the van for considerable lengths of time or just using it for short trips.

Lastly, do you prefer a modern or vintage van? Vintage vans, of course, come with lots of character and really lend themselves to conversions that use vintage and reclaimed materials as part of their design. They're the ultimate aspiration of many camper van enthusiasts and they usually hold their value, as long as they are well looked after. However, with age comes unreliability and I think you have to be a reasonably experienced mechanic to own and drive a vintage van. Vintage vans also don't have modern conveniences such as power steering and air conditioning, which make a big difference to the driving experience.

On the other hand, newer vans are so much easier to drive and much more reliable yet lack the character of vintage vans. It's up to your personal taste and circumstances as to whether you opt for new or vintage, but

remember that if you are doing the conversion yourself, you can give even a brand-new van its own character with your interior design choices – materials, colours, patterns and more. Some people might consider this the best of both worlds, to have a reliable modern camper van that you have designed yourself with the best layout for your lifestyle and an interior that reflects your taste and personality.

ABOVE *Lea Wölk and Philip Steuding's camper van (see pages 150–157) is a former fire truck. They have prioritized its off-road capabilities and installed a highly functional kitchen.*

BELOW LEFT *My own van, a new Volkswagen Crafter (see pages 42–53), is easy and comfortable to drive. What it lacked in character we have tried to make up for with a warm and personal Scandi-style interior.*

OPPOSITE *Retro textiles and tableware bring colour and pattern to the brand-new interior of the Bateses' van and are also perfect for summer picnics. Small accessories such as these can make a big difference to the overall look of your van and give you the flexibility to experiment with different palettes, especially if you have a neutral backdrop.*

# CHOOSING A STYLE

With any interior design project, I always recommend that you start by identifying your own core style, and designing a camper van is no exception. What kind of colours, eras, shapes or textures are you drawn to? Do you like a clean, minimal look or are you a maximalist at heart? There is nothing wrong with looking to the latest trends for inspiration, as long as you don't lose sight of your own preferences – the things that make your heart sing and make you feel happy and relaxed. No interior has to be purely functional, and even a small van has the capacity to be a wonderful retreat.

There are countless interior styles to choose from. Here are a few that particularly lend themselves to camper vans. They can either be used alone or combined with other styles for a personal twist. Understanding the different options is the first step toward creating your own unique sanctuary.

# RUSTIC

Simple yet full of character, rustic style is often found in farmhouses, barns and surf shacks in surroundings where natural materials are in plentiful supply. It is perfect for homes with children and pets, as rustic furniture can take plenty of wear and tear and usually looks even better for it.

Rustic interiors are defined by their use of organic materials such as wood and stone. These are often left unfinished so that they appear rough, uneven and heavily textured. Fabrics used for rustic interiors also have natural origins – popular choices include linen, hemp and sisal. The colour palette is inspired by nature: the green of the grass and leaves, the brown of tree bark and earth, the ochre of sand and sun and the beige of clay and stone.

For a number of reasons, the rustic approach is a great choice for camper vans. Firstly, the organic palette sits harmoniously with the colours you will see outside the van. This helps to blur the boundaries between inside and out and make you feel immersed in your surroundings. Secondly, the hard-wearing qualities of rustic furniture and fittings mean that the inevitable knocks and bumps of van life will not spoil the look of your interior. Thirdly, van life is intrinsically linked to living in harmony with nature. It's all about respecting, not wasting, resources and living as sustainably as possible. Rustic style is the truest embodiment of this philosophy.

THIS PAGE & OPPOSITE *Rustic, tactile textures add life to any design scheme. Rough, uneven surfaces will make the interior feel warm and inviting; you can use them throughout your space for a purely rustic design, or as a counterpoint to smoother and more streamlined elements – imagine the pleasing contrast of a shaggy rug next to a high-gloss kitchen cabinet. The tactile materials seen here include calico curtains, hemp rope and macramé, all of which are inexpensive to buy and will complement wood and stone.*

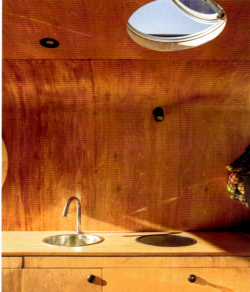

# SCANDINAVIAN

Nordic countries typically have very long, dark and cold winters, so this interior style
is all about maximizing natural light as much as possible while also making spaces feel
cosy and inviting. Scandi style has become very popular in the UK, where I live,
as more light and warmth are always needed here, too.

Pine is a key material in Scandinavian interiors, as it grows copiously in northern Europe and is light in colour. Windows are kept large to let in lots of sunshine, and walls and floors are often painted white to make them more reflective. Furniture is unfussy and minimal in style. The palette comprises neutral hues such as white, grey, beige and black, with the addition of natural greenery in the form of houseplants. Texture is more important than colour in Scandinavian design and this is highlighted by the use of another common local resource, sheepskin, for cosiness and texture along with chunky blankets knitted from sheep's wool. These textiles can be layered up on a sofa or bed to create a cocooning feel.

Scandinavian style is a straightforward, neutral base that you can make your own. It is the easiest thing in the world to add your design ideas to a Nordic interior without worrying about colours, textures or patterns clashing with one another. This simplicity of form, impressive adaptability and emphasis on natural light make the style a very popular choice for camper van interiors.

THIS PAGE & OPPOSITE *The key to the Scandinavian approach is consistency. Try to use the same type of wood throughout the space and a limited range of materials. The view out of the window should be the focal point, with the emphasis on making the best use of light at all times and using textures to create a cosy ambience. All other design elements – colour, form, pattern and line – are kept as unfussy as possible so as not to draw attention away from the natural surroundings, making this an excellent style choice for newer vans.*

# VINTAGE

In a vintage interior, care is taken to use reclaimed materials instead of new at every stage of the design process. During the building phase, this could involve sourcing reclaimed, salvaged and second-hand materials such as floorboards and doors. Later on, you can bring in antique and vintage rugs, furniture, art, lighting and textiles. These items can be found at junk shops, auction houses and flea markets or on a variety of online marketplaces; a big part of the joy of vintage is hunting down the right piece at the right price.

Vintage style is especially varied because there are so many different eras to choose from. However, if you know what your core style is, it can be fun to mix and match old pieces from different periods. Look for shapes, forms, colours, textures or patterns that link pieces together, and don't forget that lower-quality vintage items can always be painted or upcycled. For instance, I like to source French antiques for my Scandinavian interiors because their rustic textures are a great contrast to the neutral, minimalist setting – it's a style I like to call Scandi Vintage.

Once you know where to look, you may find shopping for preloved items a lot more affordable than buying new. If you are lucky enough to have a vintage van, look out for pieces from the same era that complement its design – mid-century furnishings are usually easy to find. Even if your van is new, a few well-chosen antiques will add a personal touch.

THIS PAGE & OPPOSITE *Vintage accessories lend themselves really well to styling a camper van, especially if the van itself belongs to a past era. They add colour and personality, and are a more sustainable choice than buying new. Seek out vintage fabrics for cushions/pillows and curtains, crocheted blankets and enamel tableware. Old suitcases can provide much-needed extra storage, whether inside the van or on the roof. Kitchenalia also contributes great retro style – search flea markets for vintage Tupperware, saucepans, utensils and storage tins.*

# INDUSTRIAL

Industrial style was born in the mid to late 20th century when property developers began to convert disused urban warehouses and factories into desirable lofts, apartments and other dwellings. It typically involves exposing and celebrating the architectural heritage of our cities, and giving old buildings a new lease of life. Although it originated in cavernous spaces with high ceilings, the industrial look can be scaled down to fit your van.

The building blocks of an industrial interior include bare bricks, concrete floors, steel girders and heavy-duty lighting. Wooden elements such as floorboards and beams are chunky and plain, and engineered woods such as particle board, chipboard and plywood are left exposed. Lines are straight and shapes are square, with few curves to be found. Pipes, ducts and cables are not disguised and large metal windows, usually undressed, let in lots of light. The colour scheme of black, grey, brick red and brown is derived from the hues found in old factories.

This interior style is very masculine and soft furnishings are kept to a minimum to preserve the streamlined appeal of an unadorned space. A utilitarian aesthetic, defined by a limited palette and sturdy materials, lends itself perfectly to van life. Industrial furnishings are an especially good fit for box-style vans with straight lines and right-angled corners.

THIS PAGE & OPPOSITE *If you find the industrial style too masculine or utilitarian to use on its own, it can be introduced more subtly in conjunction with the tactile materials associated with rustic, Scandinavian or vintage style such as wicker, felt, linen or wool. It is also an excellent backdrop if you want to bring houseplants (real or faux) into your design, as they will soften the harsh lines and bring the outside in. Above all, this aesthetic is an excellent choice if you need your van to be highly functional and practical.*

# MY CAMPER VAN
# JOURNEY

LEFT *We chose our previous van, a Volkswagen T5, for its tailgate back door, which provided useful shelter. Camping is the perfect holiday when you have small children. They love the sense of freedom and the shrugging off of routines. And there's nothing better than toasting marshmallows on an open fire!*

## MY EARLIEST ADVENTURES

I have always been fascinated with the idea of creating a miniature, portable home. I'm drawn to the idea of having a sanctuary, a bolthole, somewhere to call home when you're not actually at home. It's a space where you can properly relax and recharge. After a day of exploration and discovery, I love to retreat into my own haven, designed and decorated to my taste, as opposed to an anonymous hotel room. It's so reassuring and makes me feel braver and able to freely explore new places without feeling homesick. A tent, caravan or camper van is a home that you can bring with you on your adventures.

My parents bought me my first tent for my ninth birthday. It was a bright orange, nylon, triangular two-person tent, and I still remember the thrill of it being my very own space, even when it was only pitched in the garden of our house in the English Cotswolds or in the field next door. Much like having a playhouse or treehouse in the garden, it made me feel independent and free, yet safe at the same time. The magic ingredient for me with the tent was its portability, however – something no playhouse or treehouse could provide.

At around the same time, my dad was a self-employed carpenter and used a Ford Transit van for work. One summer, rather than book a holiday, my dad emptied out his van and converted it into a makeshift camper van. He created two low work surfaces down either side of the interior and attached a camping stove to one of them using a 'G' clamp. He laid down a wooden panel behind the front seats, supported by the two surfaces, and another across the seats to make two beds for me and my brother. My parents slept on the floor between the work surfaces. Once the holiday (a disaster, I recall, due to wet weather) was over, my dad simply removed everything he had installed. The holiday may have been a washout, but the seed of my love for adventure had been sown.

## CAMPING AS A FAMILY

Camping has been my holiday of choice ever since these early experiences. I eventually graduated from my beloved orange nylon tent to an ex-Girl Guide tent. I have camped in lots of places around the globe, including New Zealand and East Africa, where I remember having to check for snakes before putting the bedding into my tent! Later, my husband Rob and I bought a family tent when our three children were toddlers and introduced them to the joy of outdoor living in the UK and Europe, especially France. Camping is the best kind of holiday for young children – every trip feels like an adventure and all that freedom and fresh air is brilliant for them, plus it's one of the only affordable options if you are travelling as a family of five.

We sometimes stayed in holiday cottages, chalets or hotels instead, but they were all eye-wateringly expensive and either questionably decorated or completely bland. I don't think I would have minded spending money on accommodation nicer than our home, but it rarely was. To offset my inevitable disappointment, I started bringing along my own accessories from home, such as cushions/pillows, rugs, blankets and lighting. Once I'd spruced the place up with these favourite items and created a familiar home-from-home, I always felt a lot better!

## THE CARAVAN YEARS

As the children got older, we started looking into the idea of building a camper van. In 2010, we bought a second-hand Volkswagen Transporter T5 van in stone blue with a view to converting it into a camper van. However, whichever way we looked at it, we couldn't find a layout that would accommodate two adults and three children comfortably. With the need for five seats, every layout we considered compromised something and would have meant that we couldn't use the van for everyday driving. It was also very expensive to convert. A pop-up roof alone would have cost upward of £5,000 (around $5,800). At this point I hit on what I thought was a genius idea: instead of

converting the van, why not buy a caravan and then use the T5 to pull it? Not only would this be a lot cheaper but it would also give us the space we needed without compromising on flexibility. Of course, it couldn't be just any old caravan. What I was looking for was something with the beauty, character and quirkiness of a vintage camper van.

BELOW *I turned this scrapyard-bound 1970s caravan into a blue-and-white seaside-themed holiday home. After sanding down the exterior, I applied oil-based paint with a roller, sanding between coats to achieve a sprayed effect. I love the look of the original metal windows, which are so much nicer than modern ones made of PVC.*

ABOVE *I matched the blue of the caravan to the paintwork of our VW T5 – a factory colour called Stone Blue, which I still love. To complement the seaside theme, I had a red-and-white striped awning made to fit. I covered the inside of the caravan door with a collage of wallpaper samples, adding a protective coat of varnish on top.*

OPPOSITE *Bell tents are my favourite kind of tent for two reasons. First of all, they are the easiest to put up and can even be assembled by one person. Secondly, because they're made of canvas – unlike most tents, which are made of nylon – they don't make a rustling or flapping noise when it's windy. The result is a quiet, calm, retreat-like space that doesn't feel like traditional camping.*

After a few dead ends, in the spring of 2014 I found a 1978 A-Line Crown caravan that had been parked up and abandoned on a friend's neighbour's driveway for 30 years. Amazingly, it hadn't been towed in all that time.

I love a lot of 1970s design, but sadly the caravan was a shrine to the worst of it with its brown-and-beige interior, so I spent four months cleaning it, painting it and turning it into a characterful home-from-home. It was such a useful space – I used it as a spare room, an office and a book club venue as well as for family weekends away. However, it was difficult to tow and still not quite big enough. And Rob, who is an engineer, disliked it intensely – it was far too inefficient and quirky for him. So, after two years of fun and a few lessons learned, I reluctantly sold it.

## BELL ÉPOQUE

At this point we bought a 5m/16ft 5in bell tent, which promised the cool, homely vibe that I was looking for but with greater efficiency and practicality. Amazingly, the tent delivered on both fronts. It was generally easy to put up, pack down and transport. Moreover, inside it was nice and cosy, especially once I had furnished the interior with rugs, throws and low furniture. We holidayed in it happily for five years, taking it all over the UK and Europe.

The only time it was really hard to put up the bell tent was on a windy day, and the last time we tried to use it, in Cornwall in July 2020, was the windiest day ever. Rob and I battled with it for a couple of hours, but eventually had to give in and instead sleep in the back of the van. This was a revelation. The van was so quiet, still and comfortable compared with the tent, even with the very basic set-up of a self-inflating mattress on the van floor and everything else crammed into the front seats.

This was the nudge we needed to step into camper van territory. We began researching again and discovered the Volkswagen Crafter, a size up from our T5. We had been saving for 'The One' for a long time, so we were able to order a Crafter for delivery in January 2021.

# OUR CAMPER VAN

AT LONG LAST, WE FOUND THE PERFECT VAN – OUR TINY HOME ON WHEELS. IT'S THE COSIEST PLACE TO SLEEP AND THE VIEW CAN BE DIFFERENT EVERY MORNING.

*We knew we wanted a Volkswagen van because of the brand's reputation for reliability. There were several models to choose from, but we selected the Crafter model for its size because we wanted to install a fixed bed and a good-size kitchen and still have enough seats for four passengers. Before the van was delivered, we were a little concerned that it would be too big for us to manouevre and park easily, but we've quickly got used to it. Remember that these and similar vehicles are often used as parcel delivery vans, which seem to get absolutely everywhere, including the narrowest of lanes. At the moment our van is white and we quite like this 'stealth' look. Passers-by wouldn't necessarily notice from the outside that it's a camper van, which is very good for security.*

Our van is a brand-new 2020 Volkswagen Crafter and we arrived at this choice after much soul-searching. My heart really belongs to old vehicles – I drove a 1966 Morris Minor convertible for 10 years and my husband Rob has owned several vintage MGs. They have a lot of character and great design features. However, they can also be unreliable, slow and physically hard to drive. There are many people who really enjoy the experience of owning a vintage car or van, but you need to be up for a challenge. We had learned the hard way that we needed a reliable vehicle with features such as air conditioning and power steering and that could keep up with other traffic on the road effortlessly. We were willing to prioritize this over the looks and character of a vintage van.

My absolute priority was to have a fixed bed. My dream was to be able to sit on the bed (without having to unfold it from somewhere) with a cup of tea in hand and a dog, looking out at a beautiful view. And from Rob's perspective, a fixed bed at the back of a van allows for a roomy storage area underneath. Most van owners call this useful space 'the garage' – ours houses the electrics, water tank and various camping essentials such as folding chairs, a hammock, bikes and paddle boards.

To accommodate this vision, as well as a kitchen, a living area and seats for the driver and three passengers (now that the eldest of our three children had left home), we had to choose a long van. Fortunately, the long-wheelbase Crafter has a generously proportioned interior measuring 4.3 x 1.8m/14 x 6ft (not including the cab) and a high ceiling, which allows us to stand upright even with the insulation and cladding. Once the van had arrived, we began wrangling with all the potential layouts.

There are so many camper van conversion resources online, but our most helpful sources of information were Greg Virgoe's YouTube videos and two Instagram accounts: @vanlifebuilds and @camperdreamin. We also bought a set of layout plans from @vanlifebuilds, which gave us a head start and some general principles to follow.

As well as the layout, we thought a lot about what kind of aesthetic the van should have. I believe that any space, be it a room, shed or van, should be decorated in a way that makes you feel good and is true to your core interior style. I call mine Scandinavian Vintage – I've always been drawn to the freshness of white paint and pale wood, and I adore the character, muted colours and textures of vintage homewares. I also love to bring nature inside in the form of plants and organic materials.

BELOW  *A full-size fixed bed was a must for us. We started with two lengths of right-angle profile aluminium, which we bolted through to the side wall frame, and added five aluminium box-section profiles going widthways across the van. The bed itself is made of a single plywood sheet cut into two interlocking sections, which can be taken apart if we decide to reconfigure the van's interior in the future.*

OPPOSITE  *We can create a spare bed under the fixed bed using two identical storage cube modules made of birch-faced plywood. Our kitchen is equipped with a microwave and hob/stovetop. The fridge-freezer adds a retro touch, and what it lacks in efficiency it makes up for in good looks.*

LEFT *We built this platform to bring the rear seats up to the same level as the front seats. When the front seats swivel round to face the rear seats, this means that the living/dining-room area is all on one level. The space under the platform is also used as storage with the addition of a shallow drawer. The circular cut-out handle is a recurring motif that brings everything together.*

BELOW *Rear passenger seats do not come as standard with the Volkswagen Crafter, so we had to source them ourselves from eBay. These are actually Ford Transit passenger seats, which are a close match to our front seats. Boxing in the storage underneath is on our list of potential improvements. The kitchen divider is hollow and has pipes and cables inside.*

OPPOSITE *Formica-faced plywood for the kitchen work surface would have been very expensive to buy off the shelf, so we made our own instead. We used chrome as our accent material for the sink and splashback. The cool tone of the metal is offset by the warmth of the wood.*

I knew that the Scandinavian element of my core style would lend itself perfectly to the van. Scandi style is all about making a space feel as light and spacious as possible, and it's also big on neat storage solutions. This practical philosophy appealed greatly to engineer Rob, who had the job of implementing everything. Scandi design also makes the most of natural resources that are abundant in Nordic countries. For this reason, we chose to clad the walls of the van with oiled pine tongue and groove, which is light in colour yet exudes warmth. For contrast, we lined the ceiling with black felt and fixed wooden battens over it with shadow lines in between, which conveniently left space for LED lighting.

We built the kitchen from scratch using a lightweight timber framework with drawer fronts and cupboard doors in birch-faced ply. The work surface is made from a thicker piece of plywood topped with white Formica.

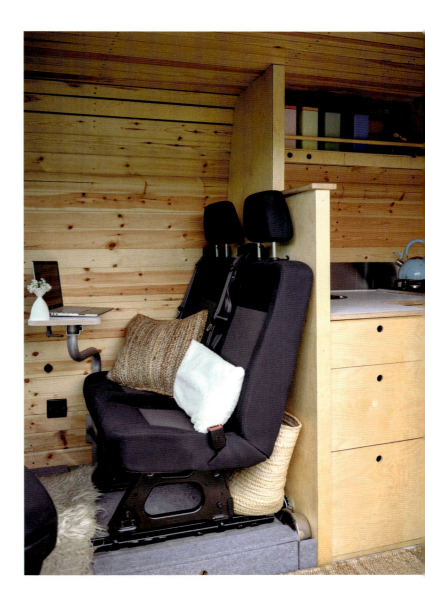

LEFT *Our van is a wonderful place to sit and read. The great thing about camper vans is that they can be thought of as spare rooms when parked on your driveway. You could use your van for sleeping, working or just somewhere to go when you need some peace and quiet. If you're considering buying a van to convert, thinking of it as an extension to your home can help to justify the cost.*

This might sound like too much wood, but the different tones and textures, including the visible layers in the plywood, create interest without competing and aid the harmonious flow from bedroom to kitchen to seating area.

Sometimes a camper van can look like a kitchen on wheels, so I was keen to avoid this by making our kitchen look less like a typical kitchen. Instead, the three 'rooms' are all designed using the same materials and are clearly zoned with partitions made of birch-faced plywood.

We routed out small round holes in the kitchen cupboard and wardrobe/armoire doors to act as streamlined handles and used this circle motif throughout to soften the sharper angles of the interior, such as the windows. We kept to black for light fittings and taps/faucets, and used chrome as the accent metal, which means that the factory-standard black and chrome of the dashboard and seats blend in with our design choices.

We tried to balance form and function by building in as much hidden storage as possible. Any visible storage has the same colours, textures and form as the other furnishings. This neutral base also means that I can add accent colours using bedding, cushions/pillows, tableware and rugs and then ring the changes simply by switching these accessories. I also really enjoy using bags and baskets hung from hooks as storage. It sounds simple, but in my opinion beautiful bags are works of art and should be used to decorate a space and add a touch of French chic, as well as for their practical function.

The real test of any camper van design, though, is to actually use it and our first trip taught us that our bed design at the back of the van wasn't suiting our needs. On our return, we built two large, movable storage cubes that could form an extension to the lower bunk. The cubes make useful coffee tables or seats both inside and outside the van, or they can be removed entirely. We also extended the fixed bed using an extra piece of plywood that slides out from under the mattress. This doubles as an extra work surface in the kitchen. I'm really happy with this solution, as it is both multi-purpose and aesthetically pleasing – the perfect marriage of form and function.

ABOVE *The passenger seat area of the van doubles as an office or dining space, thanks to a retractable table. Although it's important to carve out as much storage as possible in your van, there's no reason why this can't be visually appealing. Hanging fabric bags from hooks is a great way to add colour, pattern or texture. The drawers in the clothing storage section of the van are not fitted, so we can simply take them into the house to be packed before a trip and then pop them back into place, where they are hidden behind a door. The multipurpose storage cubes balance form with function.*

The finished interior is true to my core style, makes the space look bigger than it actually is and meets all our practical needs, too. Most importantly, though, it allows the views from outside to take absolute priority in the design. To my mind, there was no need to display much colour or pattern inside the van, as there is usually so much beauty and variety to appreciate in its surroundings – whether we are looking out at the seaside, mountains, river or countryside. Instead, our Scandi-style sanctuary on wheels is in perfect harmony with the enchanting light, colours and textures of the outside world.

LEFT *It's very often the case that reality doesn't quite match up to your dreams, but if anything I'd say that van life has exceeded my expectations. Sitting in the back of a camper van with a cup of tea while admiring a new view really is as wonderful a feeling as I had hoped it would be.*

## VIEWS FROM THE VAN

### Favourite campsite?
'Trevedra Farm in Sennen Cove, Cornwall. It boasts 180-degree sea views and has access to a secluded beach and the magical South West Coast Path.'

### Most unforgettable adventure?
'Our biggest adventure in the van so far was also our first – a three-week road trip exploring Croatia, Italy and Switzerland.'

### Item you couldn't travel without?
'The Maxxair fan at the front of our van, coupled with the roof vent at the back, is absolutely essential for keeping cool at night, especially when we're touring Europe in the summer.'

### Your design inspiration?
'It always comes from nature and from established interior styles that are defined by nature, such as Scandinavian design. Marrying this aesthetic with items I already own and love to create a functional, well-designed sanctuary is always a challenge, but is also one of my greatest pleasures in life.'

### Best thing about van life?
'Without a doubt, it's having the ability to drive your home-from-home away with you at short notice and be experiencing a new place or a new adventure within hours. Your home may be tiny, but the garden is enormous.'

# HOME ON
# THE ROAD

# BACK TO LIFE

DIY EXPERT MAX McMURDO HAS REVIVED A 20-YEAR-OLD AMBULANCE AS A UNIQUE, ECO-FRIENDLY CAMPER VAN WITH AN INDUSTRIAL-STYLE MODULAR INTERIOR.

Former car designer Max McMurdo is now a television personality known for his ingenious upcycling projects, many of which have featured shipping containers. Watching him convert one into a garden office on *George Clarke's Amazing Spaces* on Channel 4 in 2012 was the first time I'd seen a container reinvented as a building, but now they can be seen everywhere in the form of cafes, offices and even small homes. Max actually lives in a shipping container on a houseboat these days. When time on his hands during lockdown coincided with the opportunity to buy a 20-year-old Mercedes-Benz Sprinter ambulance for only £1,500 (around $1,800), he was at last able to fulfil a long-held ambition of building his own camper van. Its transformation is a testament to Max's out-of-the-box thinking and practical engineering skills.

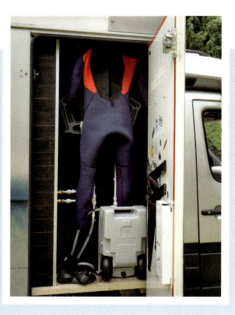

THIS PAGE & OPPOSITE *To save on the costs of a respray and to keep the van looking authentic to its age, Max has partially covered both sides of the exterior in a vinyl wrap depicting an ocean scene based on a painting by a friend. He has been able to utilize the existing storage space on one side, a throwback to the van's former life as an ambulance, as a place where he can store his wetsuit and water tank. This leaves valuable space inside for a host of clever features. One of these is a pull-out table, complete with handy built-in jars for herbs and spices, on which Max can fire up his portable pizza oven.*

Underwhelmed by his experiences of coach-built motorhomes in the past, Max wanted to design a layout that would use the available space as efficiently and attractively as possible and make the most of current technology. In particular, he wanted all the internal fittings – the bed, the kitchen and the storage compartments – to be easily removable. This would allow him to empty the van and use it for other purposes if needed. Meanwhile, he would also be able to transfer the modules themselves into other spaces.

To lend itself to this versatile design concept, Max knew that the base van would have to be box-shaped and straight-sided. The ambulance, a 2 x 3.6m/ 6ft 7in x 11ft 10in rectangle, fitted this brief perfectly.

Once the ambulance had been gutted, insulated and cladded, Max laid out and built the modules for the industrial-style interior in his workshop in Bedfordshire. Panels of strong and waterproof oriented strand board (OSB) were cut to size and then slotted into standard-size aluminium profiles. These modules were subsequently clipped into the van using aluminium rails.

Inside the ambulance, Max mounted an infrared heated panel on the ceiling as the most energy-efficient option for a small space. He also installed lightweight lithium batteries, which last much longer than traditional lead-based batteries. Finally, he affixed a set of 380W solar panels to the roof.

THIS PAGE *Owing to its straight sides, the ambulance is wider at the top than many vans, allowing for a full-length double bed across the back. Curtains and extra blankets make it a cosy place to sleep. Being able to lie on the bed with a cup of tea in hand and look out at the view through the back doors has been a revelation to Max – as it so often is to new camper van owners when they first experience this way of travelling.*

Painting the wall cladding white has lightened the space and makes the van appear wider, a useful visual trick in any space. Chrome rails with 'S' hooks hold useful, interchangeable and attractive storage options, such as canvas pockets, a chrome pot and a string shopping bag. The combination of textures makes the space interesting to look at as well as functional.

THE WAVES ARE CALLING AND I MUST GO

ABOVE & RIGHT  *A last-minute addition to the van was this table that pulls out from under the bed. Max finds it incredibly useful for both dining and working. The table is made from oriented strand board (OSB) and aluminium, just like the rest of the modules that make up the interior. It can be easily pushed away when not in use, leaving plenty of open space to move around in.*

This combination of power sources represents the best available technology and makes the van as self-sufficient as possible.

Max's highly practical design could easily have ended up looking too utilitarian, but in fact the natural wood texture of the OSB softens the look of the metal frames. The effect is heightened by the shadow-lined battens on the ceiling and front wall and the painted cladding on the side walls. Too much wooden cladding can make an interior look like a shed, but it helps if you alter the style of fitting with shadow lines, which also allow the infrared heating to work more efficiently.

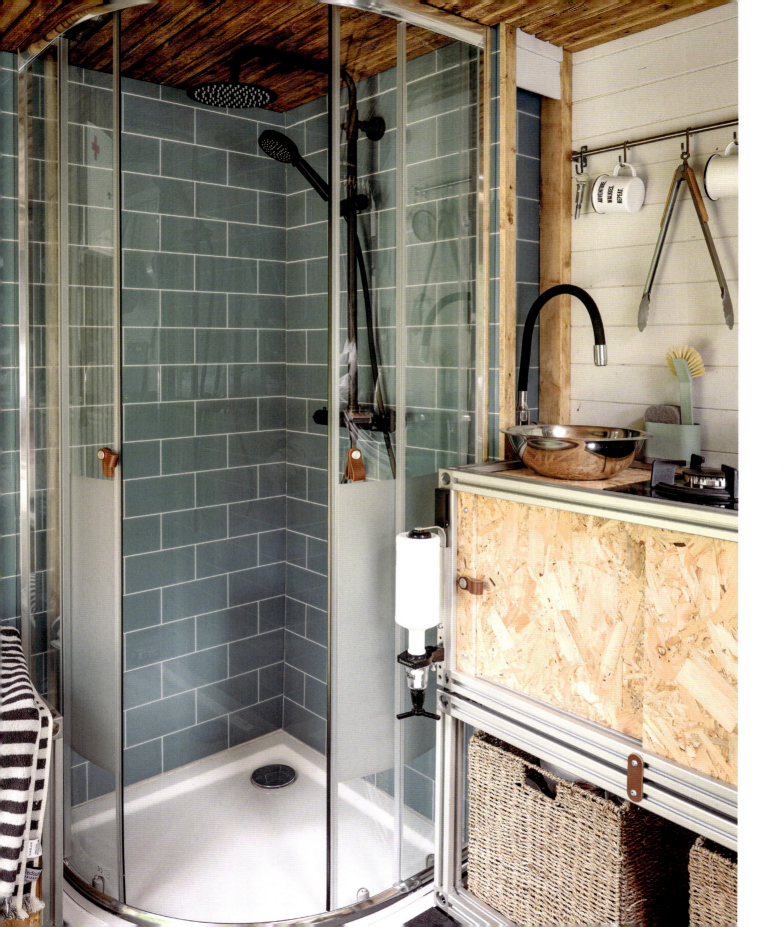

As well as the modular system, Max's other essential requirements for the van were a full-size fixed bed and shower. Most vans taper inward at the back, which means you often have to compromise on the length of the bed, but the boxy shape of the ambulance allows for a 2m/6ft 7in-long bed across the back of the van. The 2.2m/7ft 3in ceiling height allowed enough space for a full-size shower, essential for Max to warm himself up after paddle boarding and surfing. In the shower, Max avoided using heavy tiles and grouting and instead had the blue metro-tile design printed onto plastic sheeting. The finished result is very successful in that it is attractive and visually indistinguishable from the real thing, as well as lighter in weight.

Even though function has generally taken priority over form, the overall effect is of a modern yet cosy industrial space that feels like a boutique apartment. Cushions/pillows and throws are generously scattered, and a combination of basketweave and tactile grey felt storage units adds pleasing hints of texture. There are a few nods to the van's past life as an ambulance, such as the distinctive red cross on the medicine cabinet by the shower.

Max wasn't expecting to love the van and saw it as a challenge to get out of his system more than anything. However, the fact that he's been able to design it exactly how he wants it means that it's even better than he imagined. Every trip is now an adventure, and he loves to drive and sleep in the van on work trips. After all, why would you want to pay for a hotel room when you already have your own perfectly designed, self-catered hideaway on wheels?

PAGE 64 *A full-size shower with hot water was a must for Max – its enclosure houses the portable toilet, too. Fittings in the shower are black and chrome to match the kitchen next door, so everything has a seamless appearance. All the cupboards in the van have sliding doors rather than hinges, in order to save space when they are open. They also have no handles at all for a sleek, unfussy look.*

PAGE 65 *Max is a keen chef and has all his cooking utensils organized and within easy reach on the kitchen wall.*

*Everything is kept within the colour palette of black, white, grey, chrome and wood tones, with a faux houseplant for greenery. However, there is no reason why you couldn't have real plants as long as there is enough natural light inside your van.*

ABOVE *The same narrow wooden battens that cover the ceiling of the ambulance have also been oriented vertically to create a lightweight, translucent screen that separates the shower area from the cab beyond.*

# VIEWS FROM THE VAN

### Favourite parking spot?
'A little car park in south Kent where you can drive right onto the beach. There are local fish and chips for sale nearby and the beach is dog-friendly. It's a secret, though!'

### Most unforgettable adventure?
'I've just returned from an Ibiza Club Classics event played by Symphonica on Lusty Glaze Beach in Newquay, Cornwall. Hearing a live 30-piece orchestra celebrating 20 years of dance anthems was an epic experience.'

### Item you couldn't travel without?
'Without a doubt, the full-size permanent double bed with lots of storage underneath is the key to successful van life for me. It makes the van usable for longer lengths of time.'

### A trip you're looking forward to?
'I'm a big fan of rugby, so I'm planning a tour of France that will coincide with the Rugby World Cup. I'm going to take the van across the Channel and then drive around the country, watching as many matches as possible along the way.'

### Best thing about van life?
'Owning a camper van turns every day off or spare weekend into an opportunity for an adventure. I keep the ambulance on my driveway at home in Bedfordshire and it's always packed and ready to go, so I have the freedom to be spontaneous – I can just hop in and drive.'

Guy Williams has been a chartered surveyor, landlord, serial renovator and hotelier, but he's given it all up to build his dream home on wheels. Over the years, he's lived in three different vehicles: the first was a Peugeot Boxer that had been used as a prison van and the second was a Mercedes-Benz 508D horsebox from Holland, which he called The Dutchess. His current vehicle, a 2002 Iveco C1 named Valerie, has a unique interior inspired by Guy's love of skiing in the French Alps, where traditional wooden chalets are very beautiful but prohibitively expensive to buy. Fortunately, Valerie is bigger than many ski chalets, so Guy has been able to realize his Alpine ambitions, along with his dog Ethel.

THIS PAGE & OPPOSITE *Guy Williams couldn't afford to buy his own ski chalet in the Alps, so instead he bought this old horse lorry and converted it into a mobile chalet with room for up to six people. The interior is clad entirely in rustic, reclaimed wood and has been designed, decorated and styled exactly like a ski lodge. This includes the good insulation and heating that are essential in the Alps in winter and the ski-themed art and accessories on the walls. The back of the lorry folds outward to reveal a pair of French doors that perfectly frames the spectacular mountain views.*

# CHALET CHIC

A FORMER HORSE LORRY HAS RECEIVED AN INFUSION OF ALPINE STYLE FROM SKIING ENTHUSIAST GUY WILLIAMS, WHO HAS INSTALLED MANY SURPRISING FEATURES.

Guy picked up the 7.5-tonne/ 8.3-US ton lorry in late 2020. After insulating the whole vehicle, he got to work on the front section and installed two 1.8m/6ft single cabin beds, several cupboards and a wetroom with composting toilet. All the wood is reclaimed and even the roof light is an old double-glazed fridge door. Everything has been carefully calculated to be within the vehicle's weight limit.

The kitchen has been designed with full-time living in mind, so it is a good size for everyday use. The cabinets were built from an old pine dresser/ hutch that Guy picked up for £100 (around $115) from eBay; he has altered the middle drawer section to fit a Belfast sink. The floor is made from reclaimed roofing slates, which emulate the look of flagstones but without adding too much weight. Mindful of the Alpine temperatures, Guy also installed underfloor heating.

The rear section of the lorry is one of the most impressive feats of interior design I have ever seen. Two sofas, also made of reclaimed wood, have been built in on each side of the living space. These can be folded up into the walls to reveal something completely unexpected: a whirlpool bathtub set in the floor.

OPPOSITE *The living and dining area comfortably accommodates six people. The seats are strewn with cosy sheepskins for warmth and to soften the texture of the heavily grained wooden cladding. Shallow arches and curves are a recurring theme, softening the boxy lines of the interior.*

ABOVE *The kitchen is equipped for daily living with a Belfast sink and full-size electric oven. The rustic wood theme is continued with the use of an old pine dresser/hutch as the starting point for the kitchen cabinetry.*

RIGHT *As well as insulation, double glazing and underfloor heating, the lorry also has a cast-iron Hobbit log burner from Salamander Stoves for when the Alpine temperatures dip below 0°C/32°F in the winter.*

RIGHT *The front section contains two single bunks, each with its own wall light and bedding made by Guy's mother. The skylight has insulated shutters to keep this area warm and dark at night. Deep drawers have been built under the lower bed with antique brass cup handles to match those in the kitchen. The curved openings of the bunks complement the arched bathroom door on the right.*

OPPOSITE *Guy designed an electric pulley system to lower the double bed from the ceiling at night and raise it up during the day. Bookshelves with built-in ambient lighting on both sides create a cosy, personal vibe that also leads the eye to the focal point of the interior – the view out of the back doors.*

While some might think that a whirlpool tub in a camper van is a little over the top, I think it's genius – and exactly what Guy needs after a long day skiing in the Alps.

Rather than creating a separate bedroom, Guy made the most of the 2.4m/7ft 10in height of the lorry by installing a drop-down double bed. With the bed raised up, the underside becomes a ceiling dotted with 700 fairy lights, each individually mounted in tiny drilled-out holes.

The camper has not been designed for lots of touring but rather for long-term park-ups for the winter and summer seasons, so being able to move it easily and frequently was not a major concern. With this in mind, Guy has been able to utilize his extensive design and carpentry skills to create his dream ski chalet, which just so happens to be on wheels, complete with everything he needs to live his best life.

THIS PAGE & OPPOSITE *Bathing is so important to Guy that he designed the back of the lorry to accommodate an inset tub in the floor, together with an underslung 250-litre/66-US gallon water tank to fill it. Antique brass hardware complements the brass accents elsewhere. The double bed above can be lowered to a halfway point; its underside resembles a vaulted ceiling dotted with twinkling lights. Bathing here is a truly magical experience.*

## VIEWS FROM THE VAN

### Favourite parking spot?

'My favourite resort in the Alps, which has a mains electricity hook-up and ski-in/ski-out facilities. I'd love to tell you where it is, but my fellow van lifers would have me hanged, drawn and quartered if I did!'

### Most unforgettable adventure?

'I remember the day the first Covid lockdown was announced. I was at a ski resort and the van had broken down – I was waiting for a new starter motor to arrive, but it didn't show up for three months. However, I couldn't have dreamed of being stranded in a more beautiful place. Fortunately, I'd bought myself a new set of touring skis, so I had the mountains to myself, with fresh powder, friendly locals and a fully loaded Netflix account. I was in heaven.'

### Item you couldn't travel without?

'If I had to choose one, then it would be the underfloor heating. Having lived in a previous van without it, there's nothing nicer than coming back to a warm van after a day's skiing in below-freezing temperatures.'

### Best thing about van life?

'It doesn't matter where you are in the world, whether you're parked on a secluded beach or on a garage forecourt awaiting repairs – you are always at home.'

### Future plans for your van?

'After one more season in the Alps, I'm going to park it up on some land I've just bought in Cornwall. I'll rent it out to people who are interested in off-grid living or are looking for inspiration for their own van build.'

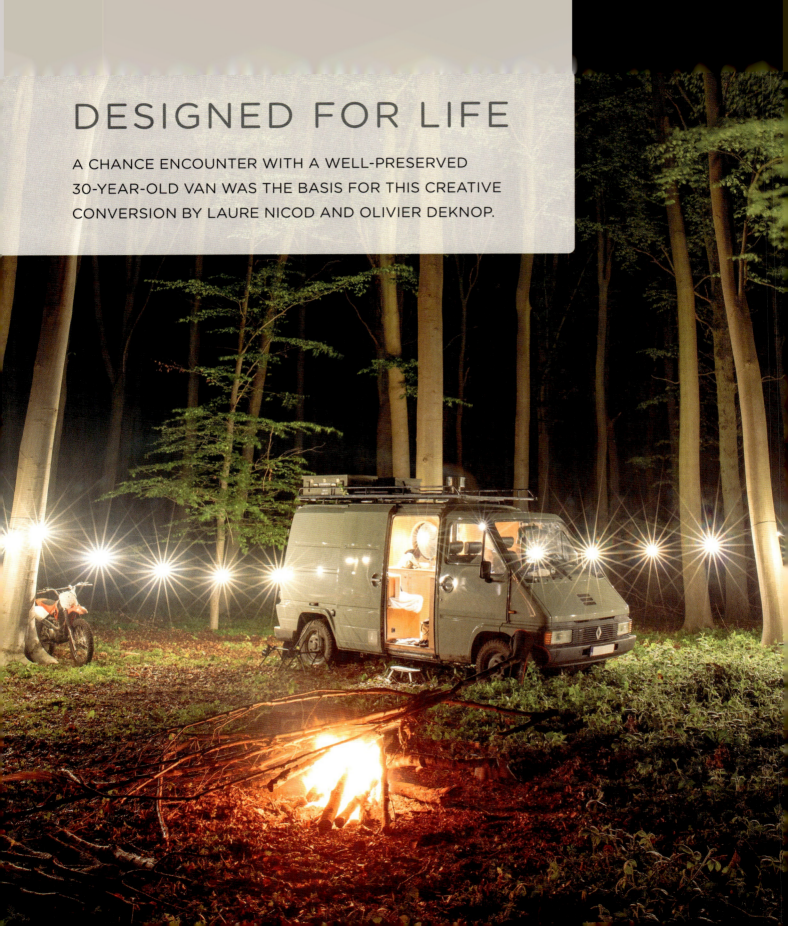

# DESIGNED FOR LIFE

A CHANCE ENCOUNTER WITH A WELL-PRESERVED
30-YEAR-OLD VAN WAS THE BASIS FOR THIS CREATIVE
CONVERSION BY LAURE NICOD AND OLIVIER DEKNOP.

THIS PAGE & OPPOSITE *The Renault van was originally white, but Laure and Olivier had it repainted in a beautiful soft green. The new colour has the effect of making the vehicle blend in with and become part of the scenery when it is surrounded by grass or trees. It also perfectly complements the all-wood interior and adheres to the nature-inspired palette drawn from its main design influences: 20th-century modernism and contemporary Japanese style. The use of black trim cleverly integrates the wheels and the roof rack into the overall look of the exterior and its sleek lines have proven to be a real asset to the design.*

Laure Nicod and Olivier Deknop are two creatives from Belgium. They randomly spotted this 1990 Renault Master 1 van in a wood merchant's warehouse in Brussels and were delighted to see that it was for sale. They felt as though it had been parked there waiting for them for years. Although they weren't specifically looking for this model of van, the couple was charmed by its distinctive sliding doors and round door handles. It was big enough to fit a double bed and tall enough for them to stand upright inside. Furthermore, it was very fairly priced, had low mileage and was in perfect condition. They even received the original sale leaflet from 1990 as part of the deal.

Laure and Olivier were also attracted by the fact that they had never before seen a camper conversion of a Renault Master and with this in mind, their challenge became clear: to take this ordinary old van and turn it into a sublime camper.

As a trained architect who specialized in interior design, Laure took a professional approach to the project. She started by creating a CAD drawing of the van so that she could begin to experiment with modelling and layouts.

The inspiration for the van's interior comes from a variety of sources, which harmonize together beautifully. The influence of modernist architecture can be seen in the minimalist, unfussy design, free of unnecessary adornments. Contemporary Japanese style is visible in the birch-ply cladding, natural elements and clean lines. Lastly, the pair looked to vintage boat interiors, which contributed the curved roof, the porthole window and the invisible joins that give the space a sealed-in feeling.

Laure and Olivier had four main priorities with the design. First of all, they were looking to build something simple and functional with a strong identity based on key design elements.

ABOVE *The camper van is laid out with the kitchen and workspace on the left and the seating area on the right. The top of the seat pulls out to form a bed that occupies the space in the middle of the van. Bedding is kept in the cupboards under the seat.*

OPPOSITE *The only kitchen utility on show in the van is the beautifully formed stainless-steel sink. The hob/stovetop is stored away in a drawer under the work surface next to a false drawer front that slides out to form a dining table or desk.*

OPPOSITE *The large porthole window is the couple's favourite design element. When pulled out, the table aligns with the window in order to make the most of the view. A cupboard door perforated with small ventilation holes is the only sign that there is a fridge present in the van.*

BELOW LEFT *A simple round sink, arched tap/faucet and circular handles complement the curved lines of the interior. Each of these elements has perfect relative proportions, contributing to the sense of harmony.*

BELOW CENTRE *The seat pads are made of foam and the cushion/ pillow covers of wool in a black, white and grey palette.*

BELOW RIGHT *Discreet lighting is embedded into the shelves, which have minimalist yet sturdy stainless-steel rails to prevent items falling off when the van is in motion.*

They wanted the space to be intimate and dark, and for the side window to take centre stage with its size, position and unusual round shape.

Secondly, Laure and Olivier were looking for a highly functional, modular interior that could be changed over time and upgraded with additional elements. However, they also wanted to keep the sense of space in the van, which ruled out the use of wall cabinets as part of the design solution.

Thirdly, they wanted to be able to live in the van for up to four days off-grid. This meant designing a robust electrical system, including a solar panel, that could sustain their fridge and other electronics for this length of time.

Finally, the couple were looking for a certain amount of contrast between the interior and the exterior. The Japanese principle of *ihyou*, meaning something

unexpected or surprising, can be seen at work here, and the curved, elegant interior is certainly a beautiful and unexpected surprise in a vehicle that looks rather boxy and masculine from the outside.

Wherever possible, natural materials were used throughout the interior. The insulation is a mix of expanding cork, hemp, linen and cotton, while the units and cladding are predominantly birch ply. Even the protective wood varnish is natural, and an added bonus of having an all-wood interior is the scent of the timber, which lingers at all times.

Other materials employed in the conversion include stainless steel for the sinks and taps/faucets and black powder-coated steel for the door handles and lights. This sparse, tight palette of materials and colours reinforces the minimalistic design.

## VIEWS FROM THE VAN

### Favourite parking spot?
'A car park on the border of the Jostedalsbreen National Park in Norway, which has breathtaking valley and glacier views.'

### Most unforgettable adventure?
'Skiing in Switzerland. Despite temperatures of -14°C/7°F at night and more snow every morning, we managed to stay warm and the trip confirmed our desire for adventure.'

### Item you couldn't travel without?
'Our little stove makes all the difference. The smell, the crackling, the warmth and light make us feel cosy even in the worst weather.'

### A van lifer who inspired you?
'Olaf Boswijk and Mirla Klijn, a couple from Amsterdam who used to travel around South America in their van. He's a DJ and she's a journalist and photographer. Following them on Instagram (@thismustbethepace) sparked our search for a vehicle.'

### How does your van make you feel?
'Both on holiday and at home. Even a simple drive to the garage for maintenance feels like an escape, but we are always at home, too, especially in bad weather. We light up the stove and after a few minutes we're all warm and cozy.'

BELOW *A compact Shepherd wood burner from Anevay Stoves is used to heat the camper van and to boil water. Made of steel, it was designed for camping and has not been fixed in place, both to simplify the installation and so that it can be used outdoors.*

OPPOSITE *The large round window was custom-made to resemble a porthole. It matches the circular rooflight overhead and is an excellent focal point. Laure and Olivier even park the van in order to ensure the best view through it.*

In the end, the design and build of the van took a full two years, including pandemic interruptions. As with any architectural project, Laure and Olivier sometimes had to wait for the right material or skilled craftsman to become available. Now that they are travelling and living in the van, the couple has found clever new ways to optimize the space. They have installed an additional front bed for their dogs, an extra drawer for the gas stove and more shelves for storage. They always had high hopes for this van, but didn't imagine it could ever be so magical and so comfortable.

# RETRO LIVING

# STYLE ICON

THIS CLASSIC 1970S VOLKSWAGEN BUS BELONGS TO EMMA AND JEREMY BATES, WHO HAVE UPDATED THE INTERIOR WHILE RETAINING ITS FREE-SPIRITED FLAIR.

Although fully modernized, the interior of the van has kept the original Berlin layout of seats, kitchen and table, with the addition of an upholstered storage module that doubles as a footrest. Emma has splashed out on colourful accessories that either pick up on or pleasingly contrast with the red exterior.

When you think about camper vans, I expect the classic Volkswagen Bus is the first that springs to mind. Its initial incarnation, the T1 Splitscreen, was based on the VW Beetle, but was roomy enough to live in. The 'Hippie Bus' soon became a symbol of a freer, more nomadic existence. Around 1.9 million T1s were built between 1950 and 1967, setting the stage for its equally iconic successor, the T2. Emma and Jeremy Bates are the proud owners of a beautiful 1978 T2 Bay Westfalia Berlin camper van.

THIS PAGE *The van has been freshly painted bright red on the lower half and white on the top half and trim – similar to its factory colours. It retains its original Westfalia pop-up roof mechanism but with new canvas.*

Although the T1 and T2 are built on the same wheelbase, there are a few key differences between them. Emma and Jeremy's T2 van has a bay window instead of the previous split-front design and also a larger body size. Sadly, the original dark wood veneer and green tartan upholstery were in poor condition, so they sold what was usable and employed a conversion company to rework the whole interior. The walls are now lined with cream washable fabric and the seats are upholstered in pale grey leather.

The Bateses' first requirement was a full-size bed, instead of the three-quarter-width version often seen in Westfalia van conversions. To accommodate this, the space traditionally reserved for a wardrobe/armoire had to be sacrificed. However, as the couple planned to use the vehicle as a weekend van rather than taking it on extended trips, Emma felt that living out of bags would be absolutely fine – as long as the bags were aesthetically pleasing! The rest of the storage was replaced according to the original

layout with overhead lockers and kitchen units in high-gloss enamel. An extra, movable storage unit has been included, which doubles as a home for the portable toilet and as a footrest for the swivelling driver's seat.

One thing I especially love about this van is that it retains my favourite feature of the Westfalia Berlin conversion: the louvred glass jalousie windows on both sides. The camper van also has its original pop-up roof (with a new canvas), which not only provides much-needed ceiling height for standing but it can also be used either as sleeping space for two additional passengers or as extra storage. The Bateses use this area to keep bedding and clothing in 1970s suitcases – a storage solution that is both useful and handsome.

The floor in the living room is neutral and easy to clean, while the one in the cab is made of sisal, which provides welcome texture and contrast to the clean lines of the interior. It also picks up on the design of the beautiful bamboo parcel shelf under the dashboard – a reproduction of an aftermarket accessory that was introduced by Volkswagen in 1955.

ABOVE *The kitchen work surface folds up to reveal the hob/stovetop underneath. A retro green-and-white enamel coffee pot can be heated over the gas flame without the need for electricity.*

ABOVE *The rock-and-roll bed takes up the full width of the van to ensure a better night's sleep. Although this has meant losing some storage space, the van looks much airier as a result. Retro-looking reading lights have been installed overhead on either side.*

RIGHT & FAR RIGHT *Emma has indulged in high-end, vintage-inspired accessories for the van. This is more affordable in a small space because you only need a little of everything.*

LEFT & BELOW *The bedding, sheets and towels for the van are all stored in two vintage suitcases, which fit in perfectly with the era and aesthetics of the van. Emma has invested in a cute heart-shaped hot water bottle to keep off the chill at night.*

OPPOSITE *As well as extra standing room, the pop-up roof can provide additional sleeping space when the van is at full capacity. However, as it is usually just the two of them, Emma and Jeremy use this for storage space, keeping the living area clear.*

The palette Emma has chosen for the inside of the van – cream, wood, bamboo and sisal – reflects her love of neutral-toned interiors. However, it also presents a wonderful blank canvas and is a space where she can play with colours and patterns that might not fit in at home: boldly striped cushions/pillows, brightly hued enamel picnicware and paisley bed linen. The result is that the camper van appears to be fully equipped for a garden party at a stately home. These colourful accessories can be layered up or toned down depending on your mood.

When it comes to vintage vans, in most cases I prefer it if the original interior can be kept as authentic as possible. However, this is not always an option, so you have to be prepared to think outside the box. In my view, doing as the Bateses have done is the next best option. The new interior is modern and spacious, but the combination of the enamel paint and highly varnished oak worktops enables the interior to retain its vintage feel. It really offers the best of both worlds: a beautifully preserved and restored example of the iconic Volkswagen T2, yet modernized in a restrained and tasteful manner that allows the most distinctive elements of the original design to stand out even better than before.

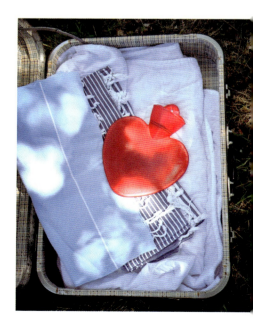

ABOVE *Plastic windows on all three sides keep the roof area from feeling claustrophobic and provide great views from high up.*

LEFT *Emma and Jeremy's grown-up children sometimes borrow the van and make up an extra bed on the upper level. The T2 Berlin was designed by Westfalia to sleep five thanks to a child-size hammock over the front seats. Though there is no hammock in this van, the fixings for it still remain in place.*

OPPOSITE *The van has no shortage of windows. The light that they let in and the 360-degree views blur the boundaries between indoors and out, making it feel spacious inside.*

## VIEWS FROM THE VAN

### Favourite campsite?

'We couldn't choose just one, because so many of them have been good for different reasons. However, what we always look for is a place with a view, be it sea, hills or woodland; something beautiful to wake up to. We often use a website called Hipcamp (formerly known as Cool Camping in the UK) to find sites.'

### How does your van make you feel?

'When we climb into our van, which we've named Rosie, it feels as if we're already on holiday. Even before we arrive at our destination, the journey is all part of it. We also get a real sense of freedom and spontaneity travelling in the van – we can change our minds, depart from the plan and set off in a different direction, which you can't always do in normal life.'

### Item you couldn't travel without?

'Installing a full-size double bed was the best thing we did when we redesigned the layout of the van. We've now got the space to get a good night's sleep – with the help of a good mattress topper, of course, which we really couldn't do without.'

### Favourite places to shop?

'We love vintage style and cheery, brightly coloured homewares, which we have sourced from markets and indie stores. It's also lovely to buy something on a trip; many items evoke memories of places we've visited.'

### Anything you'd change about your van?

'We actually can't think of a thing we'd change about Rosie – she's pretty perfect for us!'

# LA DOLCE VITA

FRENCH ARTIST BENOÎT CHOMARD FELL IN LOVE WITH POPPY, HIS VINTAGE ITALIAN VAN, AT FIRST SIGHT. THE PAIR NOW TRAVEL HAPPILY AROUND FRANCE TOGETHER.

The Italians really know how to design a good-looking vehicle and this 1976 Fiat 238 B1 belonging to French artist Benoît Chomard is no exception. Benoît found the van, which he has named Poppy, in 2016 in a barn in central France, where it had been stored for more than 30 years without being driven in all that time. Benoît, who has lived in a series of camper vans on a full- and part-time basis since 2002, decided to sell his previous vehicle, a 1973 Volkswagen T2 Westfalia, in order to buy Poppy.

THIS PAGE & OPPOSITE *Poppy is a 1976 Fiat 238 B1, still with the original blue-and-white paintwork. The compact, lightweight frame conceals an unexpectedly capacious interior, which is ideally suited for Benoît's long-distance road trips.*

PAGES 98–99 *The side entrance to the van opens up like a pair of barn doors, which houses additional built-in storage on each side. Benoît hand dyed the curtains-himself using yellow turmeric to complement the blue of the exterior.*

LEFT *Shelves and storage units are fitted above and below the window. Light filters through to the living area via holes drilled into the wooden divider.*

The Fiat 238 was produced from 1967 to 1983 and has always been very popular for camper van conversions thanks to the way it was built. Despite the small size of the vehicle, it is possible to create a surprisingly spacious living area inside because of its front-wheel-drive engine, which maximizes the available floor space. As an experienced van dweller, Benoît could see the practical advantages of this configuration. The other thing he noticed was the impressive number of windows: nine in total. For an artist with a strong appreciation of the beauty of natural light, this would make the perfect camper.

Before he could furnish the interior, Benoît first had to make the vehicle roadworthy after so many years out of use. He completely overhauled and cleaned the engine block, changed the filters, belts, pumps and seals, restored the brakes and treated all the rust spots. This was a lengthy process, but the experience of taking the van apart and painstakingly rebuilding proved to be incredibly valuable. It taught him everything he needed to know about how Poppy works, including all the odd little quirks that he would have to be mindful of on the road. This detailed knowledge is essential for owners of older vans, who will inevitably have to deal with occasional mechanical breakdowns.

ABOVE *A fixed sleeping space was not a priority for Benoît, so he designed a seating and dining area that can be folded down to form a double bed. The pendant light hanging over the table is unusual in a camper van but works very well, especially if the pendant is a plug-in that can be removed and stowed safely when in transit.*

Benoît designed and built the interior of the van himself. Instead of making detailed plans, he drew a rough sketch and let himself be guided by the materials that were available to him at the time, the tools he had access to and the extent of his own DIY skills. He insulated, cladded and whitewashed the inside walls of the van and put down a reclaimed oak floor. He then created a partition wall between the cab and the living area to improve the latter's insulation. The partition also forms the back wall to the kitchen and includes an irregular heart-shaped hatch through to the cab. The hatch provides a focal point at the front of the van and the cut-out motif is a recurring theme throughout the interior. These distinctive elements are perfect for a quirky 1970s van like Poppy.

LEFT & OPPOSITE
*These heart-shaped
chalkboard sliding doors
are form and function
defined. The cabinet
doors, drawer fronts
and table are all slightly
curved and unevenly
shaped to pick up on
the irregular curves
both inside and outside
the camper van.*

BELOW  *A stone bowl
is not the most practical
option for a kitchen
sink, but Benoît loves
it anyway. He enjoys
making the most of
whatever materials are
to hand, as shown by
the tap/faucet made
from a copper pipe bent
into an arch shape.*

As I mentioned previously, good light
is very important to Benoît, so this was
naturally a priority during his renovation
of the van. The partition wall has small
pinholes drilled into it to let rays of light
through. This is echoed in the holes of
varying sizes that punctuate the divider
between the bedroom and kitchen,
which create a magical effect when
the sun filters through.

Plenty of natural light streams in
through the windows, doors and large
skylight during the day, and Benoît
has also included plenty of artificial
illumination: ambient lamps and fairy
lights in the shelves, overhead bulbs in
the seating area and task lights in the
bedroom. Lighting can make or break
the interior design of any space and
I would argue that it's especially
important in a camper van to establish
different zones and create that sought-
after warm and cosy glow at night.

The layout of the van is constantly
evolving according to Benoît's changing
needs; he says that the secret of his
design is not to overthink it. What he
and Poppy have demonstrated is that
if you stick to natural materials such
as wood and stone and a simple colour
palette, in this case yellow and blue,
it is easy to incorporate new additions
that will soon look as though they've
been there all along.

Benoît has travelled around 25 countries during his 20 years as a van dweller. In fact, he spends so much time living out of the camper van that he has installed a letter box on the back so that he can receive his mail when the van is parked in the same place for a long time.

## VIEWS FROM THE VAN

### Favourite parking spot?
'Unfortunately, due to the new-found popularity of van life, many of my preferred places are now inaccessible – I still know a few, but they're secret!'

### Most unforgettable adventure?
'My first road trip to eastern Europe in 2003. I still remember the feeling I had when I left Aix-en-Provence and waved goodbye to the friends I was leaving behind. I felt a sense of freedom and discovery as the world opened up to me.'

### Item you couldn't travel without?
'I don't really need anything, so it's hard for me to answer. But maybe my phone – when I'm travelling alone, I like to share some of my adventures.'

### Your design inspiration?
'I don't have a particular source of inspiration – instead, I tend to just create things from ideas as they come without thinking too much. I love tinkering with tools and prefer to make the most of whatever materials are available to me at the time. As an artist, I do particularly like optimizing the natural light in all my designs.'

### Best thing about van life?
'The freedom, for sure, as well as the lessons learned. My 20 years of travel have taught me a lot, the main lesson being that it is important to remain humble and open-minded in order to experience a rich life.'

ABOVE *The kitchen and storage units were all handmade by Benoît from Douglas fir and are designed to look slightly irregular, in keeping with the character of the van. The simple colour palette of blue, white and yellow, the use of repeating motifs and the wooden surfaces throughout the van pull everything together.*

# FAR OUT VAN

THE SPIRIT OF THE 1970S LIVES ON IN SMRITI BHADAURIA AND KARTIK VASAN'S CLASSIC DODGE CAMPER, IN WHICH THEY'VE SET OFF ON AN EPIC TOUR OF SOUTH AMERICA.

THIS PAGE & OPPOSITE *Smriti and Kartik have been journeying from Canada to Patagonia in their 1977 Dodge camper van for the past two years. They especially love wild camping and have had the suspension raised on the van to allow them to travel off-road and reach more remote places. Both of them have kept their jobs (Smriti in marketing and Kartik in IT) while travelling, so a typical day involves working for a few hours in the van before heading out to explore their new surroundings. Their favourite part of the van is the cab, a homage to the original 1970s design. As Smriti says: 'It's customized to tell the story of this brown van.'*

Smriti Bhadauria, Kartik Vasan and their dog Everest have been living and travelling in their 1977 Dodge B200 Tradesman Maxi since 2020. Back in 2018, the couple was living in Toronto and looking to buy a camper van, but the modern vehicles they saw didn't feel like home to them. One weekend, on their way to a camping trip, they saw the Dodge parked up with a 'For Sale' sign on it. When they found out it had no brakes and a non-functioning engine, they initially decided it was too much of a project for them. But they couldn't stop thinking about it, and when they heard that the owner was about to list it for sale online, they knew they had to buy it and immediately transferred him the money from their campsite.

While the cab is all about retro style, the living area of the van is more about practicality and providing enough space for the couple to work, sleep and cook. They recently eschewed the popular camper van layout with a bed at the back of the van for a configuration that allows more kitchen and workspace.

RIGHT *The new design includes even more storage than before – you really can't have enough. Most of the cupboards are sleek and modern, but the couple has also included some hand-crocheted storage boxes in spice colours. These add personality and texture to the primarily neutral colour scheme.*

The couple spent two years getting ready for their trip to South America, five months of which were taken up with working on the interior. Their priorities with this first design were a comfortable bed and a large kitchen, as Smriti is hugely into cooking Indian food. Most camper vans have only a small kitchen sink, but this layout included a sink large enough to wash five pots at a time!

The couple began their road trip in August 2020 and continued to improve the van and its interior as they travelled, including two particularly large upgrades. The first one, a year into their journey, was a complete refit of

the cab based on 1970s interior images of the exact same model of Dodge, which they had found in an old magazine. They had wanted to do this in Canada, but it would have cost thousands of dollars. Instead, they waited until they got to Mexico to have the work done more affordably. As well as replicating the diamond-stitched red-leather upholstery and the original dashboard seen in the photographs, they also had the original seat fabric sewn into the design. Smriti and Kartik wanted to make the cab vibrant and retro so that anyone who peeked into their van would know that they were looking at a time capsule.

LEFT *This photograph shows the first layout that the couple installed, which was all wood. Although they liked the warm and cosy ambience, when they moved the bed to the front of the van they also introduced a lot more white into the palette to make the space feel much lighter and brighter.*

OPPOSITE *Before embarking on their journey through the US and into South America, Smriti and Kartik travelled west from their home province of Ontario, chasing the autumn colours all the way to Saskatchewan. As the time zone changed, the hues of the leaves changed, too.*

When they had been travelling for 21 months, their next project was to reconfigure the living space with a brand-new layout. There were two reasons for this. First of all, in the original layout there was nowhere for Everest to sleep when travelling on the road except for the bed and seating area at the back of the van – and he didn't like being so far away from his owners. And secondly, the couple wanted their workspace to be closer to the back door for better light and views. The solution was obvious, so the couple decided to move the kitchen from the front to the back of the camper van and bring the bed and seating area to the front of the camper van. Now, Everest can sleep directly behind them while they are driving.

The new layout includes a longer but shallower kitchen worktop that extends past the door. Not only does this make the most of previously dead space, it allows easier access to the water tanks. They installed a slightly smaller sink, but have increased their counter and storage space to make cooking easier for Smriti. The couple also painted the interior white and added lots of hooks.

It took almost two years of living in the van to show Smriti and Kartik what they really needed from it, which goes to show the importance of flexibility when you embark on this lifestyle. Everyone will make mistakes and there is no such thing as the perfect design, but your van can and should evolve over time to suit your needs.

# VIEWS FROM THE VAN

### Favourite parking spot?
'The Alabama Hills in California, the pristine beach in Todos Santos, Mexico and a campground near an active volcano in Guatemala have all been truly memorable.'

### Most unforgettable adventure?
'The kindness of people all over Latin America has blown our minds. There have been countless encounters with strangers who have invited us home, given us shelter for days and treated us like members of their own family.'

### Item you couldn't travel without?
'The kitchen and all of my Indian spices, staple ingredients and pans. Cooking and sharing food is so important to us and has hugely influenced the design of our van.'

### Favourite camper van recipe?
'One of our go-to dishes that we love to cook while travelling is Palak Paneer. It's made with spinach and paneer, which is similar to cottage cheese. Fortunately, the ingredients have been easy to find in the countries we've visited so far, although sometimes under different names!'

### Best thing about van life?
'The freedom. The moment we finish our work for the day and switch off our laptops, we are in a new destination and ready to explore. Every day we can see a new place, interact with a new culture, try a new cuisine and practise a new language. What more can we ask for in this life?'

# CREATIVE CAMPERS

# FREE REIN

JOSEPH ORPEN PUT HIS WOODWORKING SKILLS TO USE IN THIS INVENTIVE HORSEBOX CONVERSION, WHICH HE AND HIS WIFE SIAN HAVE IMBUED WITH RUSTIC CHARM.

Joseph and Sian Orpen are a couple united by their love of the outdoors. Joseph is an aspiring hedge layer who carves beautiful items from the surplus wood removed during the process, and both he and Sian have a strong appreciation of craftsmanship, camping and nature walks. This gave them the idea of finding a large vehicle to convert into a camper van where they could live full time, using rustic and reclaimed items where possible. When they spotted a 1987 Mercedes 811D horsebox in a barn in Nottinghamshire, close to where they lived at the time, they knew they had to buy it. They named the horsebox Sam Robin after Joseph's sister and the friendly robin that kept them company in the early days of the build.

THIS PAGE & OPPOSITE *The couple completely rebuilt the wooden exterior of the horsebox using scorched Siberian larch. They then added reclaimed French doors at the back, which open out to take in the view. The exterior metal parts of the van and the cab are painted dark green. The Orpens' cat Lenton travels everywhere with them and enjoys peering out of the vintage porthole in the bedroom at the front of the van. His favourite place to be, though, is the driver's seat of the sunny cab.*

Work to restore the horsebox began in February 2018, just as the cold weather front known as the 'Beast from the East' moved in from northern Europe. The first job was the complete replacement of the floor and wall cladding, which had rotted. Joseph used Siberian larch for the walls and, to protect the surface from the elements, employed the ancient Japanese wood-scorching technique of *shou sugi ban*. His passion for traditional methods set the tone for the whole restoration.

When building or renovating a camper van, you have to bear in mind that any excess weight can damage the suspension or axles. Luckily for Joseph and Sian, the horsebox has a payload of 7.6 tonnes/8.4 US tons, so they could use the rustic materials they preferred, such as reclaimed oak floorboards. There are vintage portholes, too – one was salvaged from a Boston lobster boat – and a set of full-size French doors.

OPPOSITE *Joseph constructed the sofa out of reclaimed pine. It is a perfect fit at the back of the van and also serves as a spare bed. The upholstery fabric is a hard-wearing grey herringbone wool from Abraham Moon. All the soft furnishings in the van – including the heavy linen curtains and the velvet headboard – have been selected for their ability to shrug off damage from cat claws.*

ABOVE *The vast majority of the van's internal fittings were sourced from vintage and antiques dealers. Most of the reclaimed portholes were made by marine manufacturer Wilcox Crittenden in Connecticut. This lamp is an original Great Western Railway lantern with replacement glass.*

RIGHT *The Norwegian Jøtul wood-burning stove is the heart of the van. Joseph welded plates to its feet and bolted them to the slate-topped platform so that the stove remains in place when the van is in motion. The space underneath doubles as log storage and, when empty, as another hidey-hole for Lenton the cat.*

PAGES 120 & 121 *Joseph built the kitchen from scratch – it's made entirely from reclaimed wood. The kitchen worktop was once an old door and the Bakelite handle remains in place as a nod to its former role. An antique French copper jam pan has been repurposed as a sink and is teamed with unlacquered brass taps/faucets. A wall-mounted rail made from hammered copper piping continues the warm metallic theme, which is perfect for a traditional interior. The antique heavy-gauge copper kettle on the stove was made by Benham & Froud, a London-based firm established in 1855. An original horsebox window is framed with rope and log slices and inlaid with beachcombed china fragments – a fascinating mix of materials that works wonderfully together. The faded china picks up on the blue tiles in the kitchen, which bring in a hint of colour.*

LEFT & OPPOSITE *The breakfast-bar area receives plenty of natural light through the window, which is fitted with reclaimed French louvred shutters. The shutters and skylight are framed with wood from old ammunition boxes, tying in with the rustic theme. It is the attention to detail and repeating motifs that make a space look properly designed. The painting on the wall above the window is called* The Dream – Event at Portheras Cove, West Penwith *by Sarah Vivian and is a depiction of Joseph and Sian's favourite beach in Cornwall.*

The internal layout was dictated by several factors. The couple are keen on cooking, so a proper kitchen, with a full-size oven and hob/stovetop, was at the top of their list. A functioning bathroom with hot and cold water was also a must. The space for a bedroom already existed over the cab, so this left the back of the horsebox completely free for Joseph and Sian to create a living room where they could enjoy the views out of the rear doors. Last but not least, the couple had to make space for their cat Lenton.

Once the horsebox was watertight and the layout was settled, Joseph was able to indulge in one of his favourite hobbies: hunting down reclaimed and vintage bargains. On eBay he bought a batch of Second World War ammunition boxes, which he planned to dismantle and use as cladding for the inside of the van. Although he and Sian loved the look of the old wood, complete with its original typography, they realized quickly that using it all over the interior would make it too dark. With this in mind, they resold most of the boxes and used the remaining ones to accent pine tongue-and-groove panelling painted in Annie Sloan's Old White, which helps the ammunition-box wood stand out as a design feature.

Upon entering the horsebox, you are transported into an idyllic farmhouse kitchen. Reclaimed brass taps/faucets and a sink made from a French vintage jam pan sit effortlessly on the worktop – this was originally a Georgian door and still has its original doorknob. Copper pans hang on matching rods that Joseph has made out of scrap metal and even the wall tiles are vintage. The kitchen carcass is made of leftover wood from the floor and the drawers are old crates of various sizes.

There are no straight lines in the horsebox, so it would never be possible to give it a modern, streamlined interior. Instead, the van lends itself perfectly to a rustic country decorating style. Joseph and Sian have actually made a design feature of the uneven lines by using rope and carefully selected lengths of wood from hedge laying to cover up joins and gaps. Evidence of this patchwork approach can also be seen around the original horsebox windows, which are lined with sea glass and china fragments that the couple have picked up while beachcombing.

OPPOSITE & ABOVE *Joseph has introduced a curve in the bedroom partition wall, which is lined with rope to match the windows and joints elsewhere in the van. The curve brings some softness into the space and also beautifully frames the reclaimed porthole in the bedroom. The van's neutral palette of heavily textured materials with copper and brass accents continues into the bedroom to seamless and harmonious effect.*

'This van comes into its own in winter,' says Joseph, who goes on to say that there is nothing he and Sian like better during the colder months of the year than taking a long walk and then curling up on the sofa together. It sounds like an idyllic scene, especially when you imagine flames flickering in the vintage Jøtul wood burner, which Joseph describes as his favourite item in the van, and a hearty supper bubbling away on the stove.

Although the Orpens have a new home in Devon and no longer intend to live in the horsebox full time as they did before, it will always be a special place for them – their very own sanctuary, filled with happy memories. Favourite works of art, family photographs and travel mementoes decorate the space, adding to its intensely personal vibe.

OPPOSITE *There is plenty of room for storage under the cabin bed and baskets have been added into this space to help organize it. There is also a full-size cupboard next to the bathroom – one of Joseph's handcrafted brooms hung up on the reclaimed door signals its function.*

LEFT *The entrance area sets the tone for the van's interior. As you hang your coat on one of the rustic wooden hooks handcrafted by Joseph, you can admire the heavily textured timber*

*cladding on the wall and the vintage brass light switches. Everywhere you look, there is evidence of the Orpens' remarkable attention to detail.*

ABOVE *The warm, rustic feel continues in the bathroom, which has a full-size shower made from exposed raw copper pipes and a matching shower head sourced from Etsy. Raw brass taps/faucets echo the ones that appear in the kitchen. Rope has been used again to line the joins between the walls and ceiling.*

**LEFT & BELOW**
*Converting the horsebox to a home on wheels has been a labour of love, and is a tribute to Sian's supreme planning and layout skills and Joseph's highly accomplished craftsmanship. Joseph is training in dry stone walling and hedge laying, both of which provide materials and inspiration for his beautifully made pieces. As well as useful household items such as brushes and brooms, Joseph carves exquisite spoons out of wood and has inlaid some of them with tiny ammonite fossils recovered during dry stone walling.*

## VIEWS FROM THE VAN

### Favourite campsite?

'Lower Pennycrocker Farm near Boscastle in Cornwall is a campsite we love, which has been running since the Second World War. It is located in an Area of Outstanding Natural Beauty and is blessed with the best sunsets.'

### Item you couldn't travel without?

'Our Jøtul log burner. After long winter walks, there's nothing better than lighting the fire and getting cosy. It also dries our boots and clothes if we get caught in the rain.'

### Your design inspiration?

'Our van's interior has been inspired by our love of the outdoors and rustic craftsmanship. Everything is authentic to the way we live and the origins of the horsebox.'

### Most enjoyable walk?

'Our favourite route without a doubt is the South West Coast Path in Cape Cornwall, especially the magical section that takes you from Sennen Cove to St Just. May is the best time to walk there, when the wild garlic is in full flower.'

### Best thing about van life?

'We never really feel like we're truly inside the truck. As outdoorsy people, we felt it was important to take away the barrier of a door to the outside. We achieved this by replacing the solid back door of the horsebox with fully glazed French doors. Now, when we reverse up to a forest or a sand dune, we feel a strong connection to the landscape.'

# REMOTE WORKING

THE BOHEMIAN DÉCOR INSIDE HATTI WEBSTER'S VAN
REFLECTS HER LAID-BACK, ADVENTUROUS LIFESTYLE,
WHICH EMBRACES THE FLEXIBILITY OF FREELANCING.

Hatti Webster is a keen snowboarder, surfer and hiker who took to van life early, buying her first camper van and setting off on her travels at the age of 22 when she was straight out of university. She soon learned that she had a real affinity for the lifestyle. In 2020, after a few years working in marketing in Bristol, she bought and renovated her second van, a 2010 Mercedes-Benz Sprinter with a medium wheelbase and high roof. Hatti now lives and works in her camper van as a freelance blogger and marketeer, and is able to indulge her passion for outdoor pursuits: surfing in the summer and snowboarding and hiking in the winter.

THIS PAGE & OPPOSITE  *Hatti's van has a deck on the roof – perfect for catching the last rays of sunlight. Roof decks are coveted by most van owners, but they often have to be sacrificed in favour of solar panels for off-grid travel. The good news is that some solar panels are now designed to be walkable, so they can double as a roof deck. Inside the van, Hatti's kitchen is zoned perfectly by the side window. This aesthetically pleasing arrangement allows Hatti to enjoy the best views while cooking.*

When you step inside Hatti's van, you enter a bohemian sanctuary with an interior space that measures 6 x 2.4m/ 20 x 7ft 10in. She has used the classic combination of whitewashed pine on the walls and white-painted plywood for the cabinetry, but has changed it up on the ceiling with red-cedar cladding – her favourite aspect of the van's interior. This mix of natural wood tones and textures, together with twinkling fairy lights, a bamboo-framed mirror and macramé accessories, continues the relaxed and inviting boho vibe.

Hatti comes from a family of foodies and loves to cook from scratch. Her kitchen is a thing of beauty with a large pine worktop, a three-ring hob/stovetop and plenty of ingenious storage, all framed by a large window. Metal accents include copper piping used as a stay for bottles, jars and her extensive tea supplies, copper handles for the storage units and brass hooks and screws attached to the red-cedar cladding on the ceiling. The warm tones of copper and brass help to maintain a cosy atmosphere, unlike chrome, which can look cold and functional.

ABOVE *Hatti is a big fan of tea and stores her favourite varieties within easy reach. Lipped shelves are essential in vans and the copper pipe rail adds extra security for the glass jars.*

LEFT *Herbs and spices are stored in a copper rack, which ties in with the metal accents used throughout the van. Keeping everything cohesive is especially important in such a small interior, which could look messy otherwise.*

OPPOSITE *Hatti has pulled the honey-toned palette together using textiles and decorative items. The art is by Steph Rhodes, whose own van is featured in this book from page 136. Postcards clipped to the fairy lights add to the relaxed, boho vibe. Hatti's mum helped to make the blackout blind/shade for the kitchen window, which is loosely secured with twine.*

## VIEWS FROM THE VAN

### Favourite parking spot?

'A little gravel car park that overlooks Lac de Sainte-Croix near the Gorges du Verdon in Provence. The views are incredible.'

### Item you couldn't travel without?

'My pull-out tap/faucet, which I use to shower outside and to wash wetsuits and muddy shoes. I also couldn't live without my cast-iron pans.'

### Earliest camping memories?

'We would spend most of our family holidays camping. Listening to the sound of rain on the roof, cooking breakfast outdoors and watching the sunrise take me back to my childhood.'

### Most unforgettable adventure?

'Last summer I was in the French Alps and it rained solidly for three weeks, so I decided to drive toward the sun. I explored the coastline from Monaco down to Cannes, found some free campsites and fell in love with the area.'

### Lessons you've learned from van life?

'There are so many amazing resources online, but try not to get bogged down – once you've got a plan, stop looking and start building. I've also learned that van life doesn't always go to plan, and that's OK. If your van breaks down, you could end up discovering a wild swimming spot or meeting some wonderful new people!'

It was important to Hatti to have a permanent seating area, as the van is also her office. The space between the bed and the kitchen has a table that pulls out from under the bed and doubles as a dining table and desk. Padded seats on either side, which double as storage, allow her to invite a friend or two over for supper without feeling cramped. The seating area has also become the perfect spot for reading and looking out at the scenery.

After living in the van for a year, Hatti decided to make a few changes to the décor. One of them was to put rattan inserts into all the previously plain white cupboard doors. Camper vans can end up looking very functional, but using woven materials such as rattan or bamboo adds much-needed texture, as well as an obvious weight saving. The kitchen now has a less-dominant appearance and blends in so much better with the rest of the van.

As Hatti says, there are always things to tweak in your camper van, but this is part of the joy of the lifestyle. 'This is the place where I feel most at home: snuggled up in my van while it rains outside, with candles burning and a cup of tea in my hand.'

Hatti's is a fixed bed with a pull-out table underneath – a popular design option in camper vans, for good reason. The bedding and pillows all complement the colour palette of the van, ensuring a seamless flow from kitchen to dining area to bedroom. The overall effect is light, harmonious and welcoming.

# THE GREAT
# ESCAPE

# MAKING WAVES

SURFING IS MORE THAN A HOBBY FOR ARTIST STEPH RHODES AND PHOTOGRAPHER MATT H-B – IT'S A WAY OF LIFE, IN WHICH THEIR VAN PLAYS AN ESSENTIAL ROLE.

THIS PAGE & OPPOSITE *There are very few external windows in the living area of the van, so this opening lets in valuable light from the cab, which Steph says is like a conservatory. She and Matt live with their two-year-old dog Santiago, a rescue from the coastal town of Lagos in southern Portugal. Santiago took to van life immediately and has his own bed in the cab, complete with built-in storage for his lead, food and toys.*

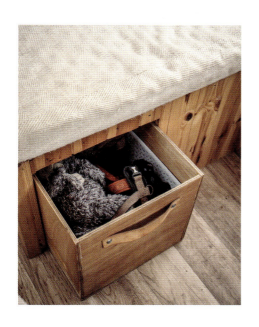

Steph Rhodes and Matt H-B are two creative souls who have travelled extensively in camper vans together over the past eight years. Steph is an artist and Matt is a surf instructor and photographer, and they tend to work in Cornwall in the summer and travel abroad in the winter. Sandy, their 1985 Mercedes-Benz Vario 613D, is Steph and Matt's third camper van. In a former life, Sandy was a police truck with a military-green exterior, but the couple has repainted it by hand in two shades of cream and sand, which make it look like it belongs at the beach. This colour choice has set the tone for the transformation of the van from functional utility vehicle to cool surf shack on wheels.

Sandy's interior pays homage to the golden palette associated with surfer culture – an outdoor way of life in which surfers typically rise before dawn to catch the waves. A classic surf shack would be simply constructed from natural materials found on the beach, such as bare wood and palm leaves. It's all about having somewhere to hang out with like-minded friends and share surfer stories, as well as having a functional space to dry your wetsuit and store your board.

It makes sense, therefore, that surfboard storage was the starting point for the layout of this camper van. To accommodate Steph and Matt's boards, the bench seat on one side of the van had to be made slightly deeper than standard. The surfboards then slide through from

ABOVE *Just as you can never have too much storage space, you can never have too many hooks – they are the unsung heroes of van living. Steph and Matt have opted for a palm-tree design, which fits in with their California surf-shack theme.*

LEFT *The doorway from the cab to the living area has an arch shape, which softens the van's chunky proportions and introduces a mid-century bohemian vibe. It also picks up on the curves of the roof and the kitchen partition wall, in contrast with the angular lines of the cabinets and the back window.*

OPPOSITE *Steph was inspired by some beautiful patterned tiles she had seen online, but was unable to source them in the UK. Instead, she purchased 44 plain white tiles for £5 (around $6) and made her own version using a stencil she designed herself and regular water-based paint. The tiles were then sealed with a protective coating of polyurethane. They bring a joyful, personal touch to the kitchen.*

the back of the van and fit snugly underneath the seat. This neat solution encapsulates surfer values – ease over elegance, but always cool and authentic.

The van has a pine ceiling with white-painted wooden cladding on the walls. The bed, kitchen and storage cupboards are also painted white and topped with pine. Bamboo and rattan accessories add texture and a mid-century twist to this calm, tonal wood palette, a nod to the beginnings of modern surfer culture in California in the 1950s and 1960s. The surf-shack look often draws on the colours, textures and materials in fashion at that time.

Steph and Matt's dreamy colour palette is a blend of terracotta, beige, peach, sand and white tones that are reminiscent of days at the seaside. Steph's artworks and hand-painted tiles add a personal element. Texture comes from the natural fibres in the curtains, upholstery and bed linen, and from the abundance of seashells. Gold palm-tree hooks are another nod to the beaches of California.

There are no windows at all in the back of the van and Steph and Matt deliberately kept it this way in order to make the bedroom space very cosy and private and the van more secure. Having fewer windows also reduces condensation, which can cause damp.

In contrast, the cab, which is separate to the main part of the van, lets in plenty of natural light through its large windscreen and side windows. Steph, who uses the cab as her art studio, says it's just like a conservatory. It's surprisingly spacious, with enough room for a bed for the couple's dog Santiago. The cab's swivelling seats were reclaimed from an old bus. Both now have beige corduroy covers, which tie in with the 1960s hippie vibe, but underneath the original moquette upholstery remains.

ABOVE *The cupboard doors have inserts made of rattan – a popular choice for bohemian spaces, as it adds texture and carries less weight visually than solid wood. Hats double as cool, textural accessories and the palm motif repeats again.*

RIGHT *The van has a generous payload, so the couple were able to opt for Shaker-style cabinets with a heavy Belfast sink and chunky wooden work surfaces that suit the proportions of the van. Caramel-coloured leather handles are stylish yet functional and are used throughout the van, working equally well in the kitchen and bedroom areas.*

To access the cab, you go through an arched doorway that Steph and Matt have created. Arches are great for breaking up boxy shapes and drawing the eye upward, and have been used throughout history to symbolize transitions and new beginnings. I think this sums up Steph and Matt's approach to life. They have carved out a lifestyle that allows them to cultivate their passions, abandon the nine-to-five and travel in search of the best surf. Their van can be whatever they need it to be – a cool home on wheels, an art studio or a surf shack. It's a truly authentic space that shows how a home created around the things you love will always be beautiful.

OPPOSITE & RIGHT *The ceiling of the van has been clad in bare pine and the walls in white-painted pine. The white gives the illusion of a wider and lighter space, and the horizontal lines of the wall cladding also have the effect of drawing your eye to the focal point of the van: the view from the back. A bookshelf is a great way to make a van feel homely, with space for mementoes as well as books.*

FAR LEFT *Matt is a surf instructor, so storage for surfboards was a key consideration when designing the layout for the van. The boards are loaded from the back of the van and fit snugly under the bed and bench seat.*

LEFT *Steph's art, which draws inspiration from the couple's nomadic lifestyle and love of surfing, is dotted around the van. The warm tones and colours of Sandy's interior – caramels, browns and peaches – are reflected in Steph's work, helping to tie the design and themes of the van together.*

**ABOVE** A dashboard needs to be functional, but in a camper van it can be homely, too. Cacti and seashells continue the boho theme, and a layer of carpet underneath stops them from rattling.

**LEFT** If you opt for a fixed bed at the back of your van, the storage space underneath is known as the 'garage'. It can be used to house all the van's utilities, such as batteries and water tanks, as well as the paraphernalia associated with your own take on van life.

**OPPOSITE** The cab has windows all around, making it a super-sunny and light-filled place to work or simply relax. Steph capitalizes on the light and space in the cab by using it as a studio for creating art. She keeps a fold-out table under her bed and her art supplies are stored in a drawer under Santiago's bed. Steph's art is greatly inspired by her and Matt's surf, sand and sun-soaked adventures.

## VIEWS FROM THE VAN

### Most unforgettable adventure?
'Our trip to Western Sahara in North Africa in the winter of 2017, back when we still had our previous camper van, a 1996 Iveco named Ivy. It was a wild ride!'

### Item you couldn't travel without?
'It would have to be our rescue dog Santie (short for Santiago) – he is the best travelling companion we could have asked for.'

### Your design inspiration?
'We first met while working in a surf shop, and our design inspiration comes from our love of surfing and beach culture. In our van we've combined earthy tones, calming colours and wooden cladding to create a surf-shack vibe.'

### Favourite parking spot?
'Anywhere in the Sahara Desert.'

### Best thing about van life?
'The sense of freedom! For us, van dwelling is about creating roots in more than one place and enjoying every moment, no matter the location. We love to be creative, explore nature and surf – we find that travelling in a van enables us to do this and gives us the freedom we are always seeking. Overall, we've learned that we're willing to make certain compromises to pursue the things that truly make us happy. We are following our passions and living with less but experiencing more!'

# BURNING RED

BALANCING FORM WITH FUNCTION, THIS EYE-CATCHING FORMER FIRE ENGINE BELONGING TO LEA WÖLK AND PHILIP STEUDING IS IDEAL FOR OFF-ROAD ADVENTURES.

Lea Wölk and Philip Steuding are two passionate globetrotters from the Thuringian Forest in central Germany. They discovered their love of travelling while backpacking as students and later they toured Europe several times with a vintage caravan that they had converted themselves. In 2019, they decided that they wanted to do a longer trip involving travel to remote places. Caravans aren't designed for off-road travel, so they started looking online for something more robust. They found a bright red 1987 Mercedes-Benz 310, which had once been a fire engine and had rear-wheel-drive off-road capabilities. Lea and Philip spent a year converting the van and eventually left home in 2020 to travel around eastern Europe for 10 months.

THIS PAGE & OPPOSITE *Outdoor living looks especially beautiful with a fire-engine-red truck. Repairing the floor and then converting the vehicle into a camper van cost £4,750 (around $5,500) and took a year to complete. The couple's focus was on functionality and sustainability. Lea's favourite part of the van is the kitchen at the front and Philip has two: the roll-up back door and the roof deck. The double hammock is the Rio XXL design by Amazonas. It's sustainably produced in Brazil using recycled cotton and, according to Lea, the most comfortable hammock ever.*

The interior of the van measures 3.3 x 1.7m/10ft 10in x 5ft 7in with a ceiling height of 1.6m/5ft 3in. Lea and Philip describe their style as Scandinavian with a Bauhaus twist. The basic principle of Bauhaus design is 'form follows function'; it's synonymous with clean, pared-back spaces and simple forms. This ethos can be seen clearly with some of Lea and Philip's design choices, for instance the double-sided Ikea Skådis pegboard that not only separates the cab from the living space but also makes organizing easy. Although function comes first, the pegboard is still a stylish piece, especially with the right accessories on display. Two smaller versions of it can be found elsewhere in the van.

LEFT *Lea and Philip love the versatility of Ikea's Skådis pegboards and have installed three of them in the van. This is the small version, which has been converted into a spice rack and kitchen utensil holder.*

OPPOSITE TOP & ABOVE *The live edge of the oak work surface is repeated on the upstand at the back where it meets the wall. Lea and Philip made the most of items they had to hand rather than buying new. For example, the kitchen sink is a reclaimed enamel bowl and the tap/faucet is made from copper piping.*

Twin sliding doors allow access to the kitchen from inside and outside the van and afford the couple both fresh air and a view while they are cooking. The large kitchen has been built using Ikea's practical and affordable Metod flatpack units. However, Lea and Philip have chosen to top the basic cabinets with a beautiful live-edged oak work surface. The warmth and texture of the wood provide a strong contrast to the flat white cupboard doors. Texture is also seen on the floor in the form of cork tiles. These have surged in popularity in recent years due to their sustainability credentials and their water-resistant and insulating qualities.

OPPOSITE & BELOW  *The fridge was bought second-hand online. Beyond the kitchen is the living and dining area, which can be converted into a bedroom. Rattan and macramé accents provide textural interest within the neutral scheme.*

LEFT  *The dining space doubles as a home office where Lea and Philip can work while on the road. The Primero Comfort HPK single-column lifting table was made by Kesseböhmer. There is still space behind the table for the couple to sit and admire the view from the open back door.*

The back of the van can be partitioned off by closing a pair of floor-length, beige linen curtains that keep warmth in at night. There isn't enough space for a fixed bed here, so Lea and Philip opted to install a table and seating area that can be converted into a bed at night. Seats upholstered in beige jumbo corduroy continue the neutral palette.

The couple chose to keep the original roll-up back door, which was still in place from the van's days as a fire engine. Although there is no view out of the van when the back door is closed, it does mean that the van is easier to keep dark and secure at night.

To make up for the lack of windows inside the van, the couple has devised an even better place from which to admire the view – a roof deck. Made of decking boards, it sits snugly next to the solar panels, the water tank and the pipes that take the solar-heated water to the shower head. Outdoor living continues at ground level thanks to a pull-out dining table at the back of the van.

LEFT *The bed is a small double, and although there is no view from the bed when the back door is closed, there are still views to be had through the side doors and front window. Philip and Lea use a floor-to-ceiling curtain to keep the bedroom dark at night.*

BELOW *The roof rack is self-built and consists of a Thule 951 base beam, steel bars and wooden planks. Watching the stars up here at night is a favourite pastime.*

OPPOSITE *In the spring of 2021, Lea and Philip's travels took them to Slovenia, where they spent a couple of weeks enjoying the beautiful scenery.*

Lea and Philip have put sustainability and functionality first at every point during the design and build of their van. The layout has worked well for them on their long trips, and despite it not being their first priority, the interior of the van looks really good, too. Overall, though, it's the eye-catching exterior of the van that really does the talking. The combination of the bright-red paintwork, the good-looking interior and the beautiful scenery of their wild camping spots is a sight to behold and makes living and travelling in a camper van look very appealing indeed.

## VIEWS FROM THE VAN

### Favourite parking spot?
'There is a wonderful wild camping spot in the Caucasus Mountains in Georgia, which overlooks Mount Kazbek on the Russian border.'

### Most unforgettable adventure?
'We took the Balkan route via Albania to Turkey, Georgia, Armenia and Iraq. On our way home via Greece, we found a one-week-old puppy and adopted him. He now travels with us – his name is Nono.'

### Item you couldn't travel without?
'Our composting toilet was supposed to be for emergencies only, but we have ended up travelling to so many remote places that it has become essential!'

### Another van lifer who has inspired you?
'We really admire a group of German camper van ambassadors called Passport Diary, which started as a blog founded by Paul Nitzschke in 2015. He now works with several other writers who share his love of the nomadic lifestyle.'

### How does your van make you feel?
'Van life for us is an opportunity to be free and to be present in the moment. It has also made us both much more aware of changes in the weather from day to day and of the cycle of the seasons throughout the year.'

# RAW MATERIALS

AN ALL-WOOD INTERIOR ON A BUDGET WAS A PRIORITY FOR DAVE AND SOPHIE GEORGE, WHO HAVE GIVEN THEIR VOLKSWAGEN T5 AN IMPRESSIVELY HIGH-END FINISH.

One of the most popular vans for camper conversions, the Volkswagen Transporter T5 was produced between 2003 and 2015. As well as being reliable and made from high-quality materials, it can sleep up to four people (with the addition of a pop-up roof) and is small enough for everyday use. It also has cultural and nostalgic value as a successor to the VW Bus. Dave George, an art-supplies shop owner, and his wife Sophie, an ecologist, bought their T5 second-hand in 2018. They had been planning and saving for their perfect van for a long time, so they knew exactly what they wanted. Storage, comfort and aesthetics were their watchwords.

THIS PAGE & OPPOSITE *Figuring out how to store everything needed for a long trip while still having a full-size double bed was a puzzle. Dave and Sophie's solution was to construct the bed with a slide-out section and a removable mattress piece that fits perfectly behind the back doors when not in use. One of the few drawbacks of the design is that the kitchen set-up requires good weather to work, but the space it saves is worth the occasional inconvenience.*

Building the van was a long process. It's so important to work out how you want to use a space before you do too much to it, and vans are no exception.

With this in mind, Dave and Sophie took their first trip in the empty van, travelling for 10 days with just a single mattress for a bed. They later added a fixed bed and a television for a holiday in Spain. However, it was only when the idea of a 'big trip' took hold that they focused on finishing the van and making it into a space where they could live comfortably for up to a year.

The couple took inspiration from vans they'd seen on Instagram that had simple wooden storage and pull-out kitchens. It was important to them that the T5's interior had an all-wood finish, but their budget was tight, so they had to work creatively with average-quality kiln-dried wood from a builders' merchant.

**ABOVE** *The space under the bed provides much-needed storage and every inch is used. Among the essential items that have found a home in this spot are Dave and Sophie's walking boots – a must for outdoor living.*

**ABOVE RIGHT** *The couple needed a vented cupboard for the split-charge fuse box/distribution board, so they added a Celtic knot design.*

**LEFT** *Books are very important to Dave and Sophie, and their library is a distinctive part of the van's interior. The design of the open shelving allows the books to be stored securely, but also puts them on display so that they are part of the décor. Creating a sanctuary for yourself, filled with the things you love, really helps prevent homesickness.*

In order to make it look more appealing, they spent a lot of time finishing and refinishing the wood with repeated sanding and staining. They accentuated the look by ageing the inexpensive brass handles and fittings using a combination of salt and vinegar. The end result of their hard work is a high-end, polished look, which appears much more than the sum of its parts.

As well as looking beautiful, the wooden storage is also surprisingly capacious. In fact, it comfortably houses two guitars, a longboard, exercise equipment, the television, a fishing rod, a cool box, a library of books, clothes and outdoor equipment and various cameras and other helpful gadgets.

The pull-out kitchen is a brilliant space saver, of course, but it does mean that all the cooking has to be done outside, rain or shine. Fortunately, Dave and Sophie mostly use the van to travel in hot countries, so this is rarely an issue.

Apart from the electrics, Dave and Sophie designed and built everything themselves, even going so far as to sew their own fitted sheets for the bed. It is a testament to how functionality never has to trump form, however small the space.

ABOVE As the ultimate plan was to be able to live in the van for over a year, the couple didn't want to leave behind anything that would make them yearn for home. As a result, storage had to be found for their two guitars, one acoustic and one electric.

OPPOSITE With careful planning and attention to detail, Dave and Sophie have achieved a balance of form and function. Their van is equipped with everything they need for long adventures, yet it is also a restorative space that they never tire of looking at or spending time in.

## VIEWS FROM THE VAN

### Favourite parking spot?
'Anywhere in the French Alps. The whole region is so well set up for van adventures and it's wonderful to have access to such an incredible landscape.'

### Most unforgettable adventure?
'Dave's favourite was our stay at the Sierra Nevada ski resort in Spain, where we spent a few days skiing and snowboarding while living in a van that resembled an igloo. Sophie's was the north coast of Scotland due to her fondness for bogs, mist and epic mountain climbs.'

### Item you couldn't travel without?
'Some people might roll their eyes at this, but honestly it's our 12-volt television. After a long day of adventure, it's great to snuggle up and watch a series together.'

### Favourite books in your travelling library?
'Dave's current pick is a collection of short stories by Haruki Murakami and Sophie's is *Wait Until Spring, Bandini*, a novel written in the 1930s by the American author John Fante. However, the most-reached-for book on our shelves is the *Collins Bird Guide*, usually right after hastily getting out the binoculars!'

### How does your van make you feel?
'That we have come home. When we first set off, we wondered how we would get used to such a small space. However, on the brief occasions when we have gone back and stayed in a house, it's actually been quite hard to settle. The van is so cosy and familiar that it doesn't matter where we are in the world; we close up the doors at night and we are home.'

# TRAVEL IN STYLE

LUXURY HOTEL ROOMS PROVIDED INTERIORS INSPIRATION FOR TRAVEL BLOGGERS STUART CONWAY AND ASHLEY McAFEE TO CREATE A BOUTIQUE HIDEAWAY ON WHEELS.

Stuart Conway and Ashley McAfee are childhood sweethearts with a passion for travel. They have been blogging full time about their adventures around Europe, Asia and America, and closer to home in Scotland, since 2018. When the pandemic hit in 2020, the couple decided to buy a van to keep their travel dreams alive. They chose a 2003/04 Vauxhall Movano L2H2 FWD with only 80,000 miles on the clock and the added benefit of a partial conversion, meaning that the electrics, insulation, heating and cladding were already done. The existing layout with the bed at the back, kitchen at the front and dining/office space in the middle was also perfectly usable, so the couple simply had to make a few adjustments to the interior and then decorate it to their taste.

The first thing they did was to remove the existing double bed frame and install a king-size one, which is oriented lengthways instead of across the van. A comfortable bed really does make or break van living, and as travel bloggers, Stuart and Ashley are accustomed to high-end accommodation. In fact, hotel room design serves as inspiration for the interior styling of the van and for hints of luxury such as fluffy dressing gowns/bathrobes, wall-mounted soap dispensers and high-thread-count bedding.

Stuart and Ashley then painted the walls white and refitted the kitchen with white cabinet fronts and black hardware for a sleek, contemporary look.

THIS PAGE & OPPOSITE *So far, Ashley and Stuart have used their camper van only to travel around Scotland, although they have plans to roam further afield. For now, the van means being able to enjoy the beautiful views of the Scottish landscape without compromising on the luxury that staying in a hotel would offer. High-quality bedding and dressing gowns/bathrobes, together with really good coffee, elevate the experience of waking up in the camper van so that it feels as though the couple are staying in a boutique hotel – but with new sights and sounds every day.*

BELOW *The middle cupboard door in the kitchen hinges upward to form a table for two in the seating area. Ashley has chosen high-end tableware and accessories to elevate the look of the van, a styling tip that she has picked up from staying in hotels.*

OPPOSITE *The existing kitchen was looking a little tired, so Stuart and Ashley replaced the cabinet doors and sprayed the worktop with a copper colour to bring it up to date. They added a splashback of vinyl metro tiles in a stone colour to match the textiles in the bedroom and seating area, pulling the colour scheme together.*

Inspired by their travels in Bali, they installed a swing, complete with fairy lights, which hangs from the frame of the side door of the van. The swing adds a unique and fun design element to the van as well as useful extra seating, which can be stowed away at the end of the bed when not in use. When they are parked up somewhere, surrounded by nature, the swing is the perfect spot to sit, relax and take in the view.

As with all beautiful small spaces, though, true success requires inventiveness, multi-purpose design and excellent storage. Stuart and Ashley's van includes generous storage space in the 'garage' under the bed, which is accessible from inside and outside the van. The seating area in the centre of the van also contains lots of secret storage and, ingeniously, Stuart has designed one of the kitchen cabinet fronts so that it swings up on hinges to form a dining table.

With a keen eye for expensive-looking accessories and with a no-compromise policy on the king-size bed, Ashley and Stuart have created a luxury, boutique-hotel-style camper van that will suit their aesthetic and needs well as they travel far and wide in the coming years.

## VIEWS FROM THE VAN

**Favourite parking spot?**
'The Arisaig area in the West Highlands. It's home to stunning white sand beaches and has beautiful views out to the islands of Rum and Eigg.'

**Item you couldn't travel without?**
'Although we're very fond of our king-size bed, the thing we really couldn't live without is our diesel heater – an absolute necessity in Scotland most of the year!'

**What would you do differently in your next van?**
'We would definitely incorporate a shower inside – right now we have a make-do shower out at the back of the van, which is not ideal in Scottish weather. Luckily, facilities at most of the campsites we've visited have been great.'

**Best thing about van life?**
'We love slow mornings in the van, starting with those first moments when you wake up and have to think about where you are. Then opening the door to enjoy the fresh air with a coffee and a beautiful view.'

**Would you use the same interior style in a house?**
'We are just about to start renovating our first home and we love the idea of making the best use of a small space, so the van is something we will draw inspiration from. We love having a purpose for every little area.'

OPPOSITE *The couple have stuck to a palette of white and stone with accents of black and copper, creating a pleasing blend of boho, rustic and minimalist styles. Their styling nods to their travels in Nashville, Texas, the Mojave Desert and Indonesia.*

RIGHT *Inspired by the swings found hanging from palm trees at the beach in Bali, this swing is a quirky touch but still tasteful, as the materials used – hemp, wood and sheepskin – are all within the existing colour palette.*

# RESOURCES

## WALLS & FLOORS

**Annie Sloan**
www.anniesloan.com
IG: @anniesloanhome
*Upcycling expert Annie Sloan has the best range of chalk paints, which are suitable for all surfaces – minimal preparation required.*

**Beija Flor**
www.beijaflorworld.com
IG: @beijaflorworld
*Vinyl rugs in a variety of designs and colours that would suit both vintage and modern van interiors.*

**Felted Sheepskins**
feltedsheepkins.co.uk
IG: @feltedsheepskins
*Add warmth, softness and texture to your camper van with a handmade, cruelty-free sheepskin rug from a small farm in Devon.*

**Little Greene**
www.littlegreene.com
IG: @littlegreenepaintcompany
*Heritage paint colours in a choice of finishes.*

**Osmo**
www.osmouk.com
IG: @osmo_uk
*These plant-based oils are the best way to protect any wooden surfaces in your camper van.*

**Weaver Green**
www.weavergreen.com
IG: @weaver.green
*Soft rugs, cushions/pillows and textiles made from 100% recycled plastic for indoor and outdoor use.*

## HARDWARE, HOOKS & HANDLES

**Anthropologie**
www.anthropologie.com
IG: @anthropologie / @anthropologieeu
*Quirky hooks and doorknobs for a characterful camper.*

**Dowsing & Reynolds**
www.dowsingandreynolds.com
IG: @dowsingandreynolds
*Stylish door handles, taps/faucets and light switches.*

## COOKING & DINING

**Falcon Enamelware**
www.falconenamelware.com
IG: @falconenamel
*Unbreakable and stylish enamel tableware and bakeware.*

**Ooni**
uk.ooni.com
IG: @oonihq
*The coolest portable pizza ovens.*

**RidgeMonkey**
www.ridgemonkey.co.uk
IG: @ridgemonkey
*The multi-purpose Connect Combi pan is loved by many van lifers, as it allows you to cook a whole meal on just one gas ring.*

**Target**
www.target.com
*Wheat-straw tableware in pastel tones – unbreakable, eco-friendly and pretty.*

## FURNITURE & HOMEWARES

**Custom Size Beds**
www.customsizebeds.co.uk
IG: @customsizebeds
*Quality mattresses made to order in any size or shape – essential for looking after your back when camping.*

**Etsy**
www.etsy.com
IG: @etsy / @etsyuk
*Handmade and vintage homewares.*

**Flying Tiger Copenhagen**
www.flyingtiger.com
IG: @flyingtiger
*Good-value, quirky home accessories for a fun camping set-up, including hammocks and picnicware.*

**Lights4fun**
www.lights4fun.co.uk
IG: @lights4fun
*Illuminate your outdoor space with a great selection of solar, battery and mains-powered fairy lights and festoon lights.*

**Poppy and Honesty**
www.poppyandhonesty.com
IG: @poppyandhonestyuk
*Custom-made Liberty-print bedding, bags and cushions.*

**Sklum**
www.sklum.com
IG: @sklum.welovedesign_uk
*Macramé hanging chairs and other outdoor furniture.*

**Urban Outfitters**
www.urbanoutfitters.com
IG: @urbanoutfitters / @urbanoutfitterseu
*Off-the-shelf bedding and bamboo mirrors for a bohemian look.*

## CAMPSITES & PARKING SPOTS

**UK Campsite**
www.ukcampsite.co.uk
*Old-school website with reliable reviews for British and European campsites.*

**Hipcamp**
www.hipcamp.com
*An online booking platform for sites in the UK, North America and worldwide.*

**Park4night**
www.park4night.com
*A super useful app showing where you can park up for the night for free.*

**Trevedra Farm, Cornwall**
www.trevedrafarm.co.uk
*My favourite campsite in the UK, with its own beach.*

**Bel Ombrage, Dordogne**
www.bel-ombrage.com
*This site by the river in Saint-Cybranet is a well-kept secret.*

## VAN LIFE EXPERTS

### Greg Virgoe
www.youtube.com/gregvirgoe
IG: @gregvirgoe
*Essential information on all the van
conversion basics, such as insulation,
layout and electrics.*

### The Restoration Couple
www.restorationcouple.com
www.youtube.com/therestorationcouple
IG: @restorationcouple
*Step-by-step guides to all aspects of
van conversion.*

### Van Life Builds
www.vanlifebuilds.com
www.youtube.com/vanlifebuilds
IG: @vanlifebuilds
*An excellent company for bespoke van
conversions, Van Life Builds also sells
floor plans and gives a lot of help to
self-builders.*

### Camper Dreamin'
www.camperdreamin.com
www.youtube.com/camperdreamin
IG: @camperdreamin
*Another excellent company for bespoke
conversions run by experienced van lifers.*

# FURTHER READING

**Shed Style:** Decorating Cabins, Huts,
Pods, Sheds and Other Garden Rooms
*by Selina Lake (Ryland Peters & Small)*

**Surf Shack:** Laid-Back Living by
the Water *by Nina Freudenberger
(Hardie Grant Books)*

**The Van Conversion Bible:** The Ultimate
Guide to Converting a Campervan
*by Charlie Low and Dale Comley
(Independent Publishing Network)*

# PICTURE CREDITS

Key: Ph = photograph.
All photography by Dan Duchars unless otherwise stated.
All photography © CICO Books 2023 unless otherwise stated.

**Front cover** Emma and Jeremy Bates and family, vintage camper van; **endpapers** Dee and Rob Campling's own converted van www.dee-campling.com; **1** Emma and Jeremy Bates and family, vintage camper van; **2–3** Ph © A van owned and designed by Laure and Olivier of Maître Renault; **4** Ph © @the.redcamper owned and designed by Lea Wölk and Philip Steuding; **5 above** Emma and Jeremy Bates and family, vintage camper van; **5 below** Ph © Hatti Webster @thecampercreative; **6** Joseph Orpen, @rural.crafts.by.joseph; **7–9** Ph © Smriti Bhadauria and Kartik Vasan, @thebrownvanlife; **10** Ph © Benoît Chomard and Poppy of @sweetvanlife; **12–13** Ph © Andrew Jenkinson, UK caravan industry expert; **14** Emma and Jeremy Bates and family, vintage camper van; **15–17** Ph © Andrew Jenkinson, UK caravan industry expert; **18** Joseph Orpen @rural.crafts.by.joseph; **20** Ph © Max McMurdo; **21 above left** Steph and Matt – creative adventures in their van Sandy @slownsteadylivin; **21 above right** Joseph Orpen @rural.crafts.by.joseph; **21 below left** Emma and Jeremy Bates and family, vintage camper van; **21 below right** Max McMurdo; **22** Steph and Matt – creative adventures in their van Sandy @slownsteadylivin; **23 above** Joseph Orpen @rural.crafts.by.joseph; **23 below** Steph and Matt – creative adventures in their van Sandy @slownsteadylivin; **24 above** Ph © @the.redcamper owned and designed by Lea Wölk and Philip Steuding; **24 below** Dee and Rob Campling's own converted van www.dee-campling.com; **25–26** Emma and Jeremy Bates and family, vintage camper van; **28 left** Joseph Orpen @rural.crafts.by.joseph; **28 centre** Ph © Benoît Chomard and Poppy of @sweetvanlife; **28 right–29** Joseph Orpen @rural.crafts.by.joseph; **30** Dee and Rob Campling's own converted van www.dee-campling.com; **31 left** Steph and Matt – creative adventures in their van Sandy @slownsteadylivin; **31 centre** Ph © A van owned and designed by Laure and Olivier of Maître Renault; **31 right** Steph and Matt – creative adventures in their van Sandy @slownsteadylivin; **32 left** Emma and Jeremy Bates and family, vintage camper van; **32 centre and right** Ph © Benoît Chomard and Poppy of @sweetvanlife; **33** Emma and Jeremy Bates and family, vintage camper van; **34** Max McMurdo; **35 left** Joseph Orpen @rural.crafts.by.joseph; **35 centre** Max McMurdo; **35 right** Joseph Orpen @rural.crafts.by.joseph; **36** Dee and Rob Campling's own converted van www.dee-campling.com; **38–41** Ph © Dee Campling; **42–53** Dee and Rob Campling's own converted van www.dee-campling.com; **54** Max McMurdo; **55** Ph © A van owned and designed by Laure and Olivier of Maître Renault; **56–67** Max McMurdo; **68–75** Ph © Guy Williams @thefatponyworkshop; **76–83** Ph © A van owned and designed by Laure and Olivier of Maître Renault; **84** Emma and Jeremy Bates and family, vintage camper van; **86–95** Emma and Jeremy Bates and family, vintage camper van; **96–105** Ph © Benoît Chomard and Poppy of @sweetvanlife; **106–111** Ph © Smriti Bhadauria and Kartik Vasan @thebrownvanlife; **112** Joseph Orpen @rural.crafts.by.joseph; **114–129** Joseph Orpen @rural.crafts.by.joseph; **130–135** Ph © Hatti Webster @thecampercreative; **137** Ph © Steph and Matt @slownsteadylivin and @roamslowstudio; **138–149** Steph and Matt – creative adventures in their van Sandy @slownsteadylivin; **150–157** Ph © @the.redcamper owned and designed by Lea Wölk and Philip Steuding; **158–163** © Dave and Soph's self-built camper van @vanstagramage; **164–169** Ph © Ashley and Stuart @ontheroadagaintravels; **171** Max McMurdo; **173** Ph © Guy Williams @thefatponyworkshop; **176** Dee and Rob Campling's own converted van www.dee-campling.com; **back cover** Ph © Dave and Soph's self-built camper van @vanstagramage; **spine** Ph © Benoît Chomard and Poppy of @sweetvanlife.

# BUSINESS CREDITS

**Dee Campling**
www.dee-campling.com
IG: @deecampling
E: dee.campling@gmail.com
*24 below; 30; 36; 38–41; 42–53; 176.*

**Andrew Jenkinson**
UK caravan industry expert and published author of 16 books.
YouTube: Caravan Industry Expert – Andy Jenkinson
Facebook: Caravan History Books
*12–13; 15–17.*

**Benoît Chomard**
Slow travel; painting; photography; DIY.
IG: @sweetvanlife
E: sweetvanlife@projectvanlife.com
*10; 28 centre; 32 centre; 32 right; 96–105.*

**Dave and Sophie George**
Van Life
IG: @vanstagramage
*158–163.*

**Emma Bates**
IG: @emma.emmeline
*1; 5 above; 14; 21 below left; 25–26; 32 left; 33; 84; 86–95.*

**Guy Williams**
Custom van conversions and glamping site (North Cornwall)
IG: @thefatponyworkshop
Mobile bar available to hire: @thefatponysocialclub
*68–75; 173.*

**Hatti Webster**
www.hattiwebster.co.uk
IG: @thecampercreative
E: thecampercreative@gmail.com
*5 below; 130–135.*

**Joseph Orpen**
IG: @rural.crafts.by.joseph
Etsy: TheArtfulHedger
*6; 18; 21 above right; 23 above;*
*28 left; 28 right–29; 35 left; 35 right;*
*112; 114–129.*

**Laure Nicod and Olivier Deknop**
Maître Renault
IG: @maitrerenault
and
Laure Nicod – Photographer
IG: @superflou.studio
*2; 3; 31 centre; 55; 76–83.*

**Lea Wölk and Philip Steuding**
www.theredcamper.de
IG: @the.redcamper
*4; 24 above; 150–157.*

**Max McMurdo**
Designer, author and TV presenter.
www.maxmcmurdo.co.uk
*20; 21 below right; 34; 35 centre;*
*54; 56–67; 171.*

**Smriti Bhadauria and Kartik Vasan**
IG: @thebrownvanlife
*7–9; 106–111.*

**Steph Rhodes and Matt H-B**
Slow 'n Steady Livin
www.slownsteadylivin.com
IG: @slownsteadylivin
and
Roam Slow Studio – Steph's art
and illustrations
www.roamslowstudio.com
IG: @roamslowstudio
E: roamslowstudio@gmail.com
*21 above left; 22; 23 below; 31 left;*
*31 right; 137; 138–149.*

**Stuart Conway and Ashley McAfee**
www.ontheroadagaintravels.com
IG: @ontheroadagaintravels
*164–169.*

**The publishers would
also like to thank:**

**Loxwood Meadow**
Loxwood
West Sussex RH14 0AL

**Old Coastguard Campsite**
5 Enys Cottages
Pendeen
Penzance TR19 7ED

**Radwell Lake Campsite**
Radwell Mill
Baldock
Hertfordshire SG7 5ET

**St Winnow Campsite**
St Winnow Barton
Lostwithiel
Cornwall PL22 0LF

# INDEX

# ACKNOWLEDGEMENTS

I have loved every second of creating *Camper Heaven* and I would like to thank everyone at RPS and CICO for giving me the opportunity. To Jess Walton for suggesting the idea, crafting it with me and then skilfully organising the logistics of all the location shoots – no easy task at all and definitely beyond my talents! To designer Toni Kay, art director Sally Powell and creative director Leslie Harrington – I am so grateful to have been able to rely on your experience and skills. Thanks, too, to senior commissioning editor Annabel Morgan for believing in me and to editor Sophie Devlin for guiding me through the process so patiently and editing so beautifully.

Thanks to lovely photographer and excellent human Dan Duchars who shot five of the case studies with me – Our Camper Van, Back to Life, Style Icon, Free Rein and Making Waves. We had such fun shooting those camper vans on location and huge thanks to all of the owners for allowing

us into your precious spaces and telling me all about them – it was such a privilege and I hope we did them justice for you.

We weren't able to shoot all the case studies ourselves, so thanks, too, to the rest of the camper van owners who supplied their own fantastic shots of their pride and joys and answered my many questions so thoroughly and thoughtfully.

Thanks, too, to my dad for passing on his of love and extensive knowledge of vintage vehicles to me and to caravan and camper van guru Andrew Jenkinson for his help with A History of Van Life and for supplying the vintage photographs. What my dad doesn't know about old vehicles and what Andrew doesn't know about caravans and camper vans isn't worth knowing!

Finally, thanks to my children Anna, Immy and Theo, who are my world, and to my husband Rob, who always encourages and supports me 100% with my endeavours and mostly enables them, too (except for the occasional eye roll!).